I0169430

THE EARLY LITERACY COMPANY

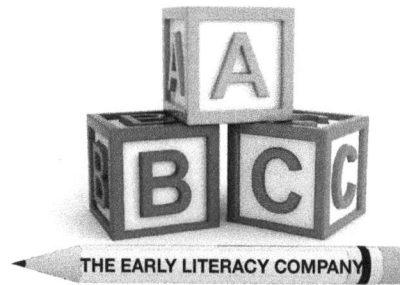

Author Gail Nordstrand, Reading Specialist.

Book Design Karen Predmore, Graphic Designer.

Conceptual Artwork Belinda Carter, Artist.

Editing Support

Maureen Peterson

Dimensions Of Letters

Learning to print progresses to the use of three lines and the lines are learned as the top, middle, and bottom lines. The dimensions of letters are formed within these three lines.

All uppercase letters touch the top and bottom lines.

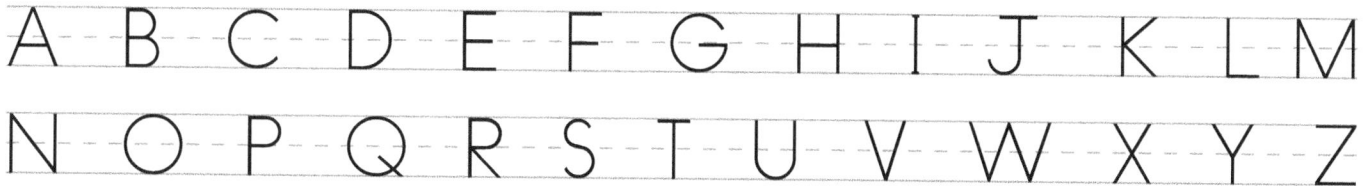

A B C D E F G H I J K L M
N O P Q R S T U V W X Y Z

Uppercase Letter Formation

These uppercase letters are made without lifting your pencil.

C G L O S U V W Z

These uppercase letters are made with two strokes by lifting your pencil once.

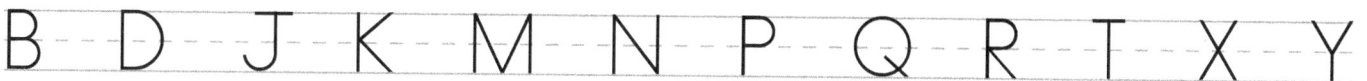

B D J K M N P Q R T X Y

These uppercase letters are made with three strokes by lifting your pencil twice.

A F H I

This uppercase letter is made with four strokes by lifting your pencil three times.

E

Demonstrate how to finger trace letter A.
Have child practice on the next page.

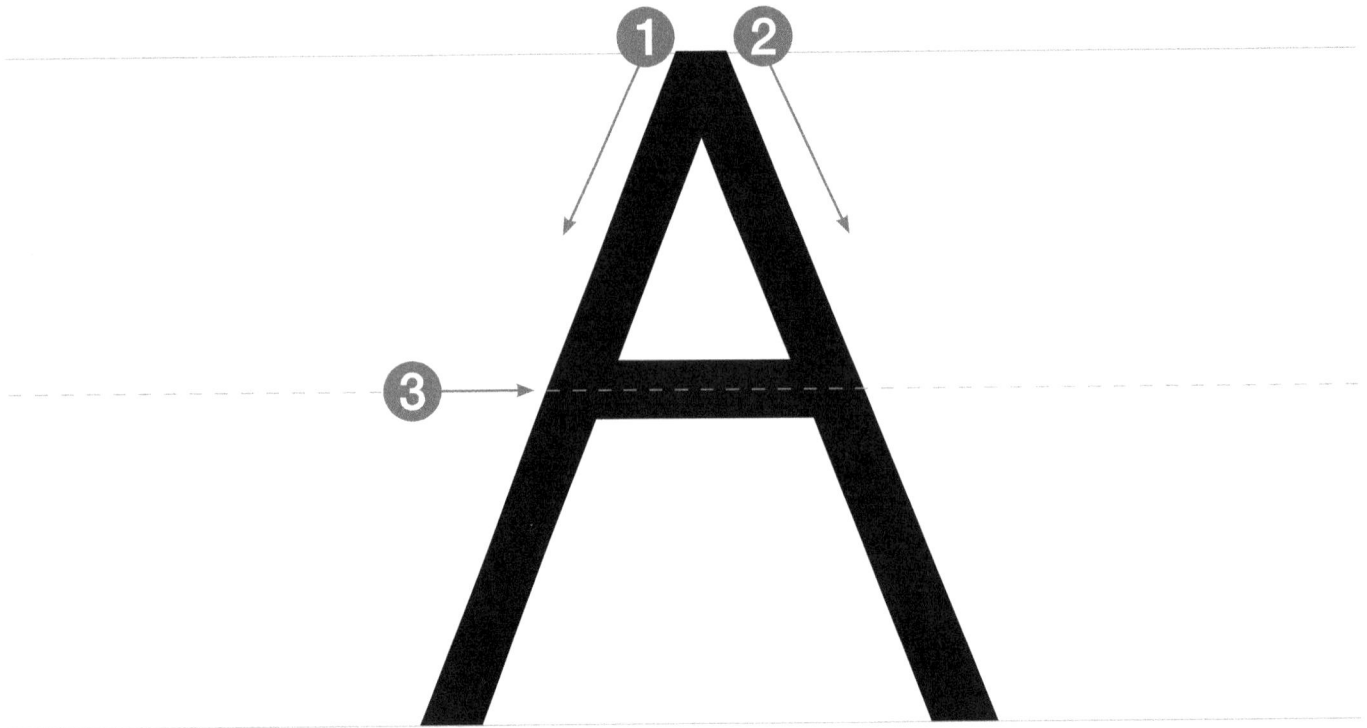

Directions:

1 Starting at the top slant down left.

Lift finger and bring back to the top.

2 Slant down right.

Lift finger.

3 Connect the slanted lines left to right on middle line.

Say verbal clue when tracing A

"DOWN ... DOWN ... CONNECT"

Have child say verbal clue as they trace the letter with their finger

"DOWN ... DOWN ... CONNECT"

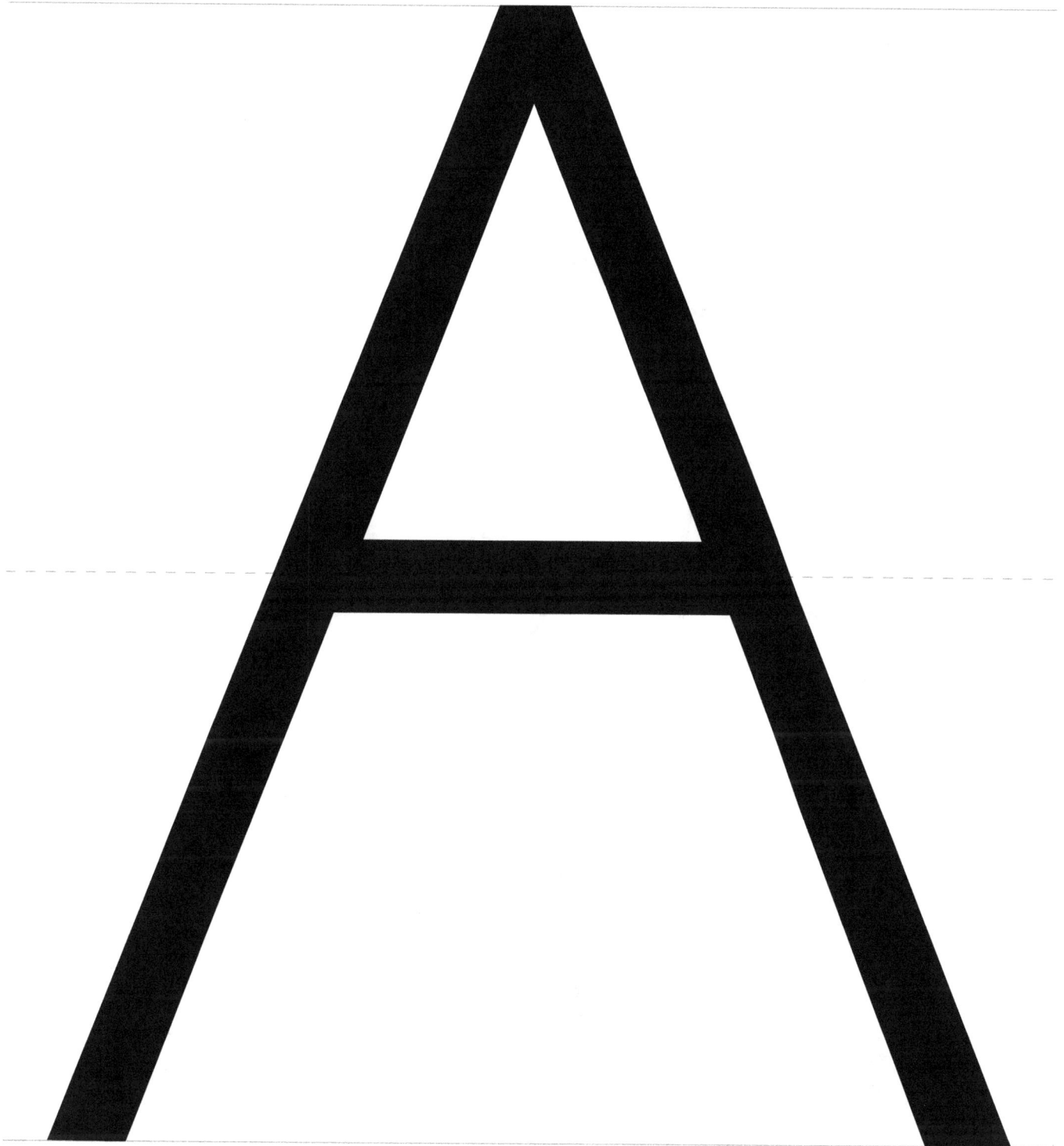

A

Trace the letters with a pencil.

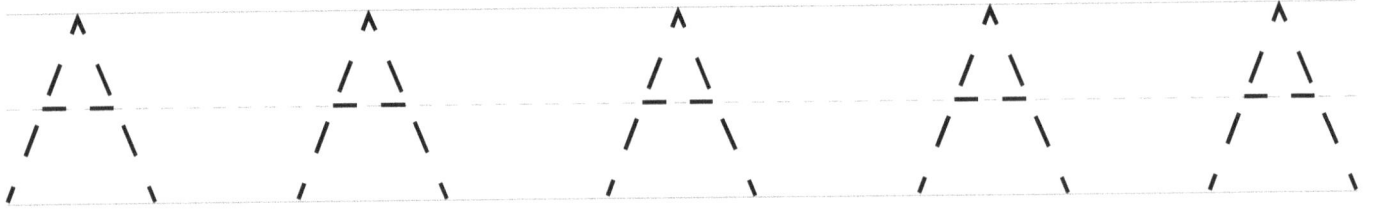

A A A A A A A A A A

Color the Alligator.

Trace A and print your own letter A four times with a pencil.

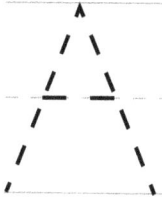

A

Draw a picture that starts with A.

Demonstrate how to finger trace letter B.
Have child practice on the next page.

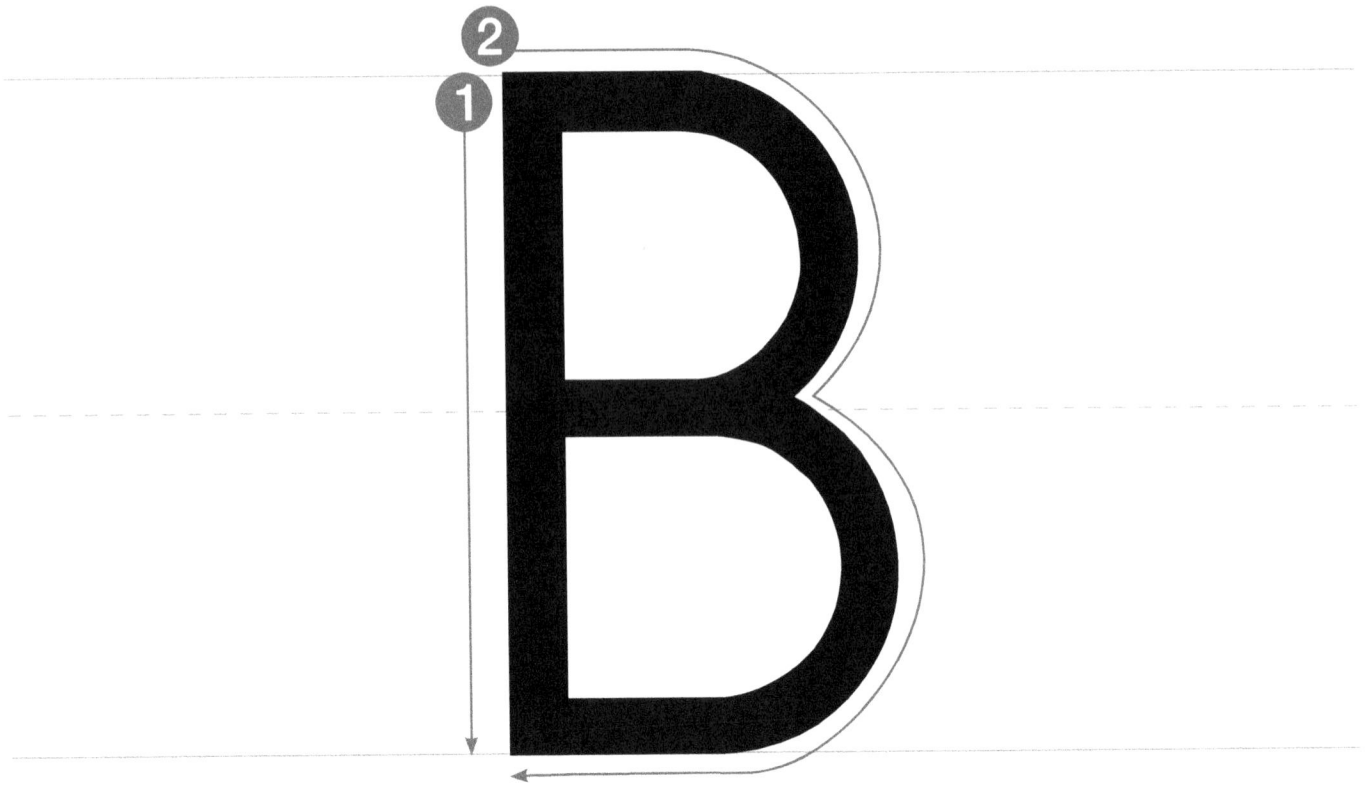

B

Directions:

1 Starting at the top go straight down.
Lift finger and bring back to the top.

2 Curve around to the middle and curve around to the bottom without lifting your finger.

Say verbal clue when tracing B
"DOWN ... BACK TO THE TOP ... AROUND ... AROUND"

Have child say verbal clue as they trace the letter with their finger
"DOWN ... BACK TO THE TOP ... AROUND ... AROUND"

B

Trace the letters with a pencil.

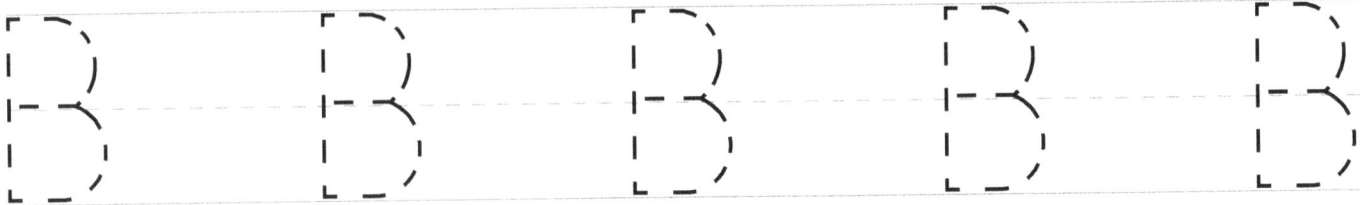

B B B B B

Color the Bunny.

Trace B and print your own letter B four times with a pencil.

B

Draw a picture that starts with B.

Demonstrate how to finger trace letter C.
Have child practice on the next page.

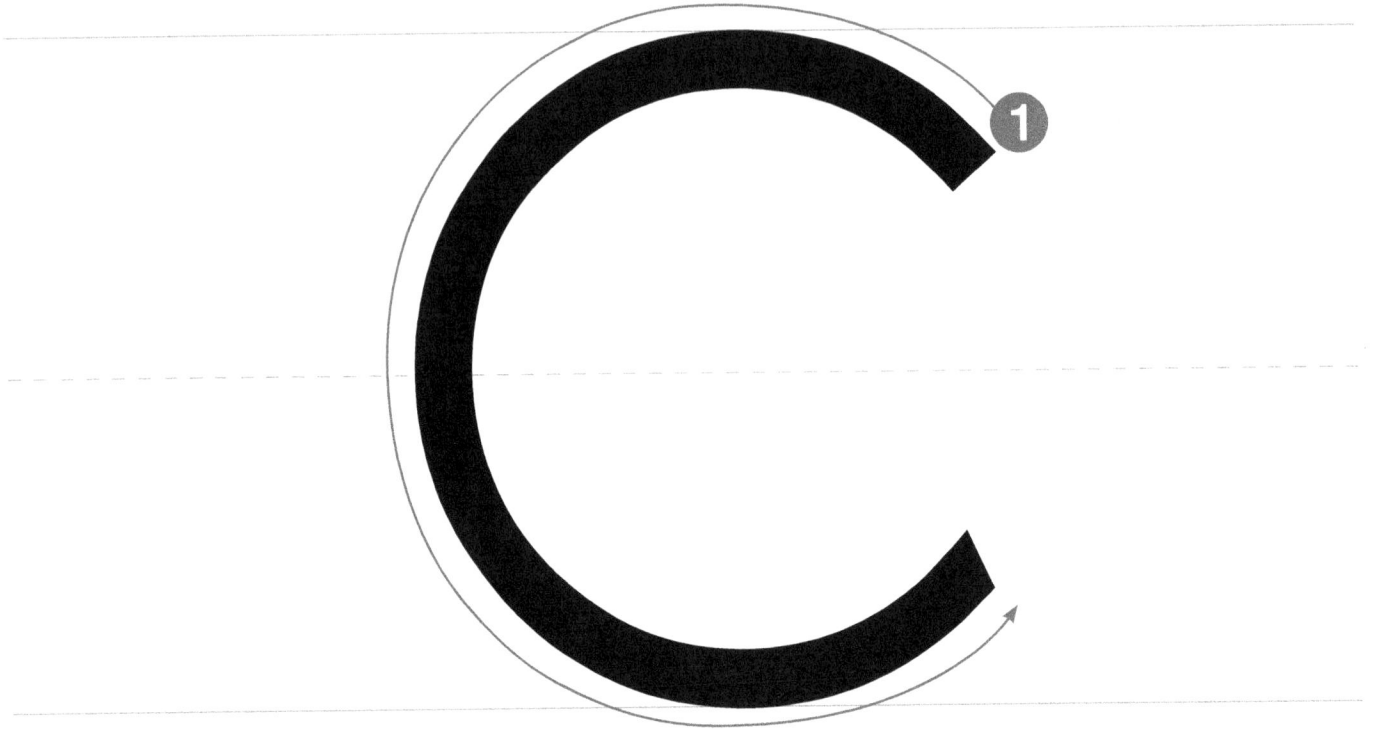

C ①

Directions:

① Starting below the top and without lifting your finger, circle left, up and around but don't close.

Say verbal clue when tracing C

"CIRCLE UP AND AROUND BUT DON'T CLOSE"

Have child say verbal clue as they trace the letter with their finger
"CIRCLE UP AND AROUND BUT DON'T CLOSE"

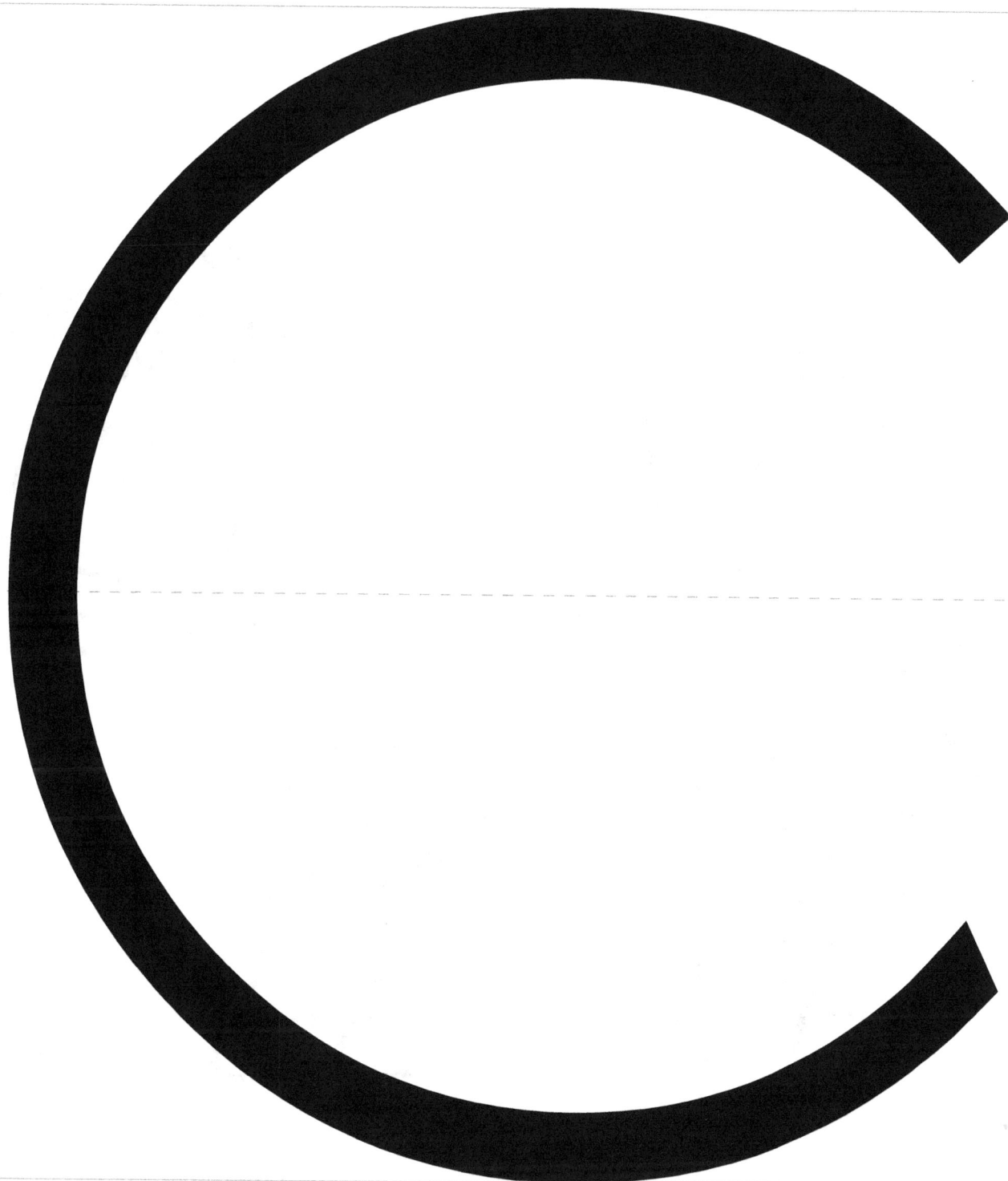

Trace the letters with a pencil.

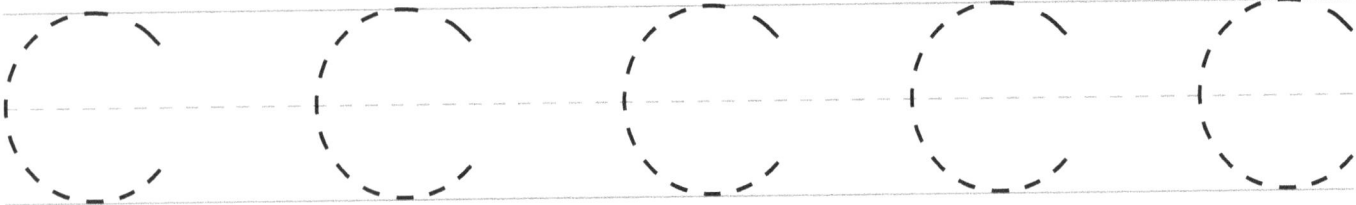

Color the Cow.

Trace C and print your own letter C four times with a pencil.

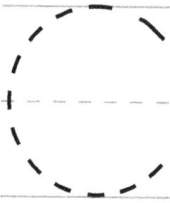

Draw a picture that starts with C.

Demonstrate how to finger trace letter D.
Have child practice on the next page.

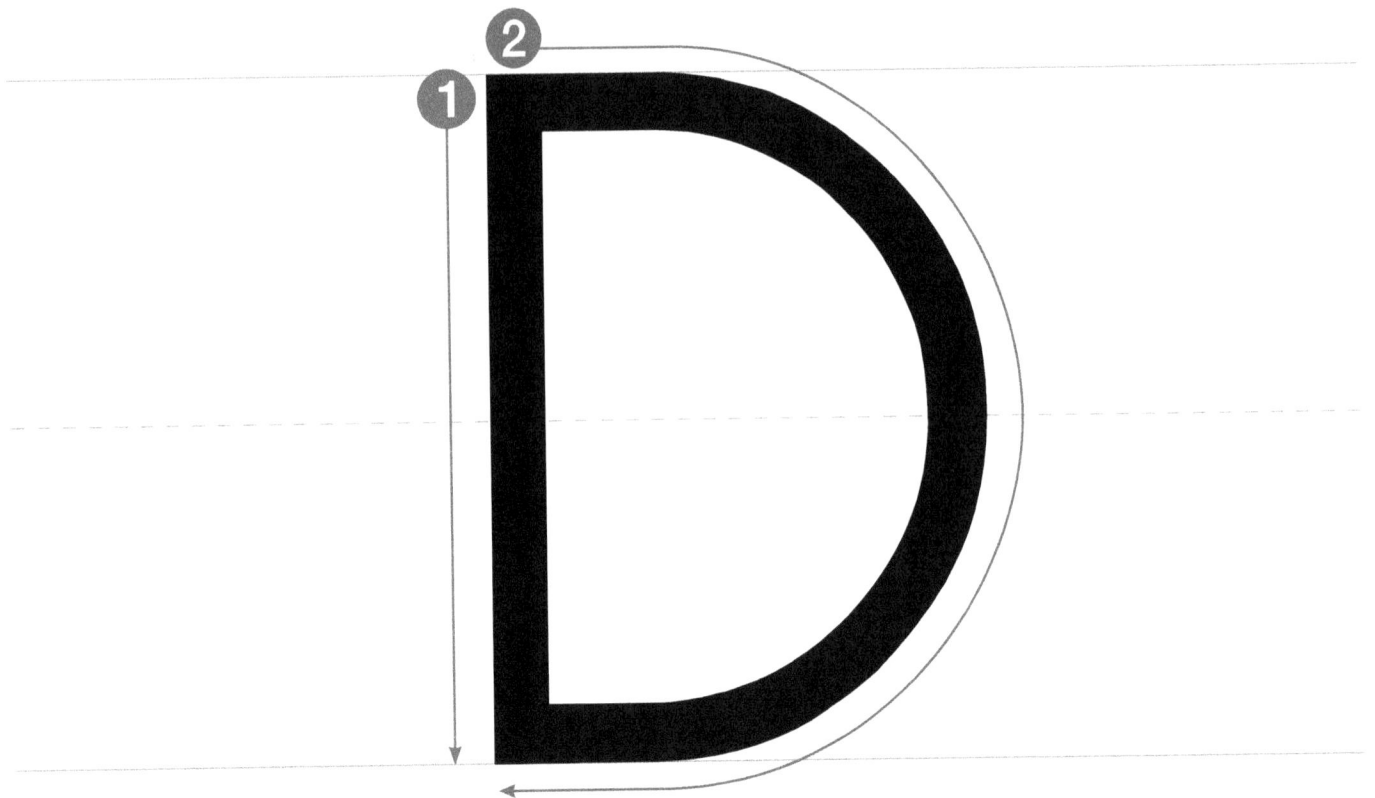

Directions:

1 Starting at the top go straight down.
Lift finger and bring back to the top.

2 Curve around to the bottom.

Say verbal clue when tracing D
"DOWN ... BACK TO THE TOP ... AROUND"

Have child say verbal clue as they trace the letter with their finger

"DOWN ... BACK TO THE TOP ... AROUND"

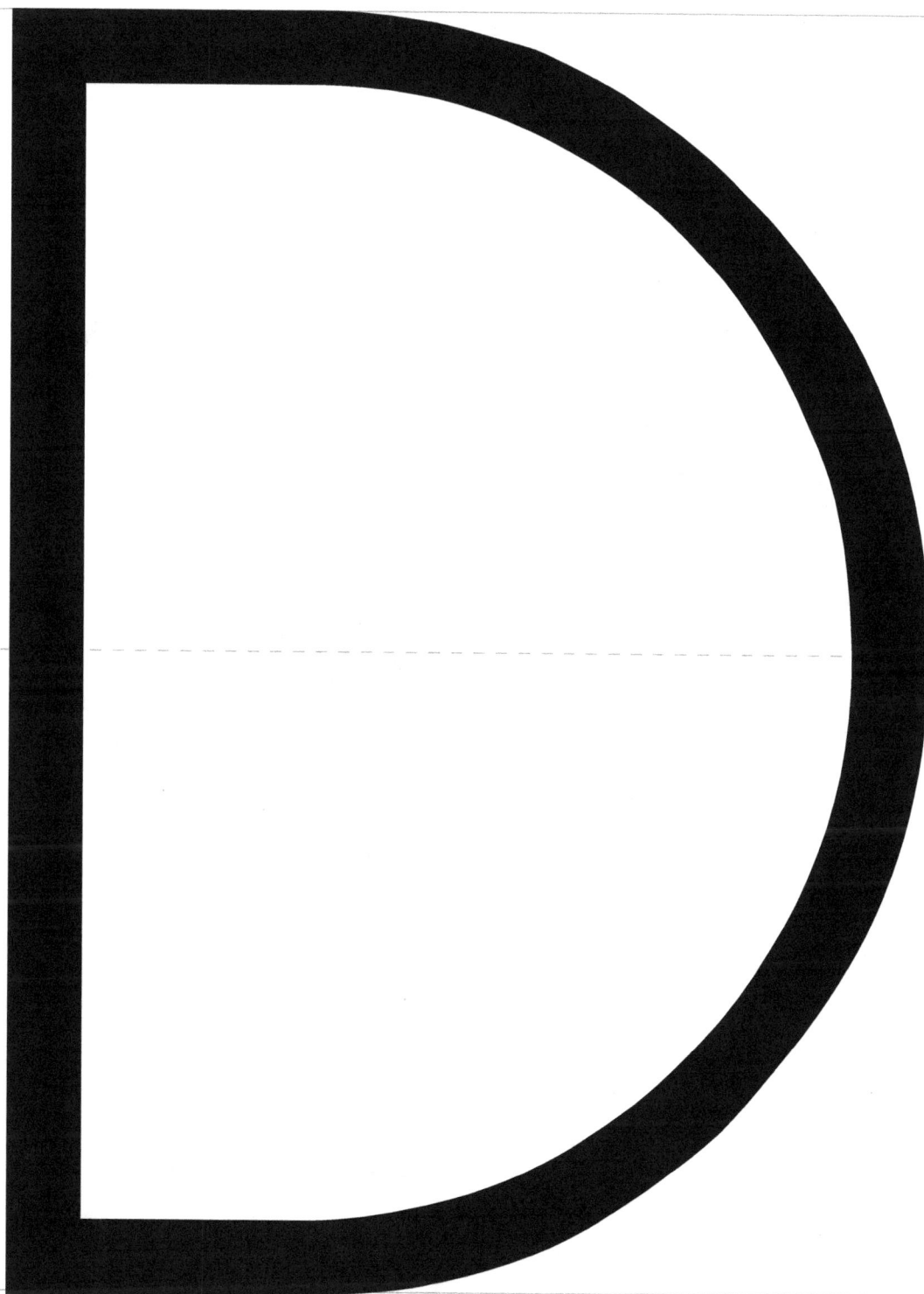

Trace the letters with a pencil.

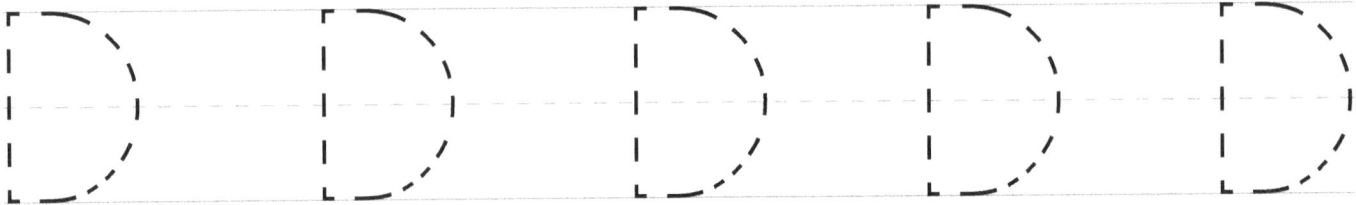

D D D D D

Color the Dolphin.

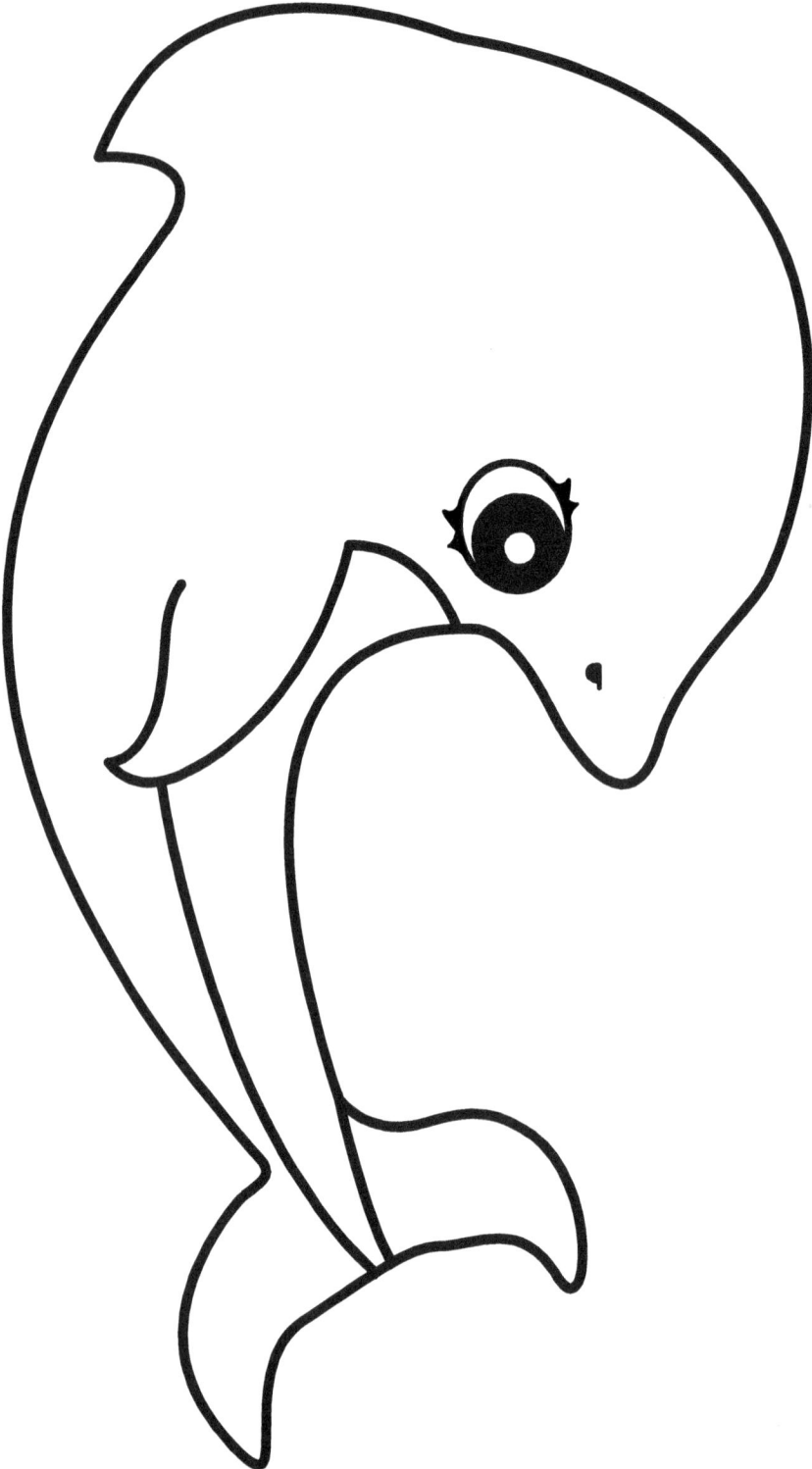

Trace D and print your own letter D four times with a pencil.

D

Draw a picture that starts with D.

Demonstrate how to finger trace letter E.
Have child practice on the next page.

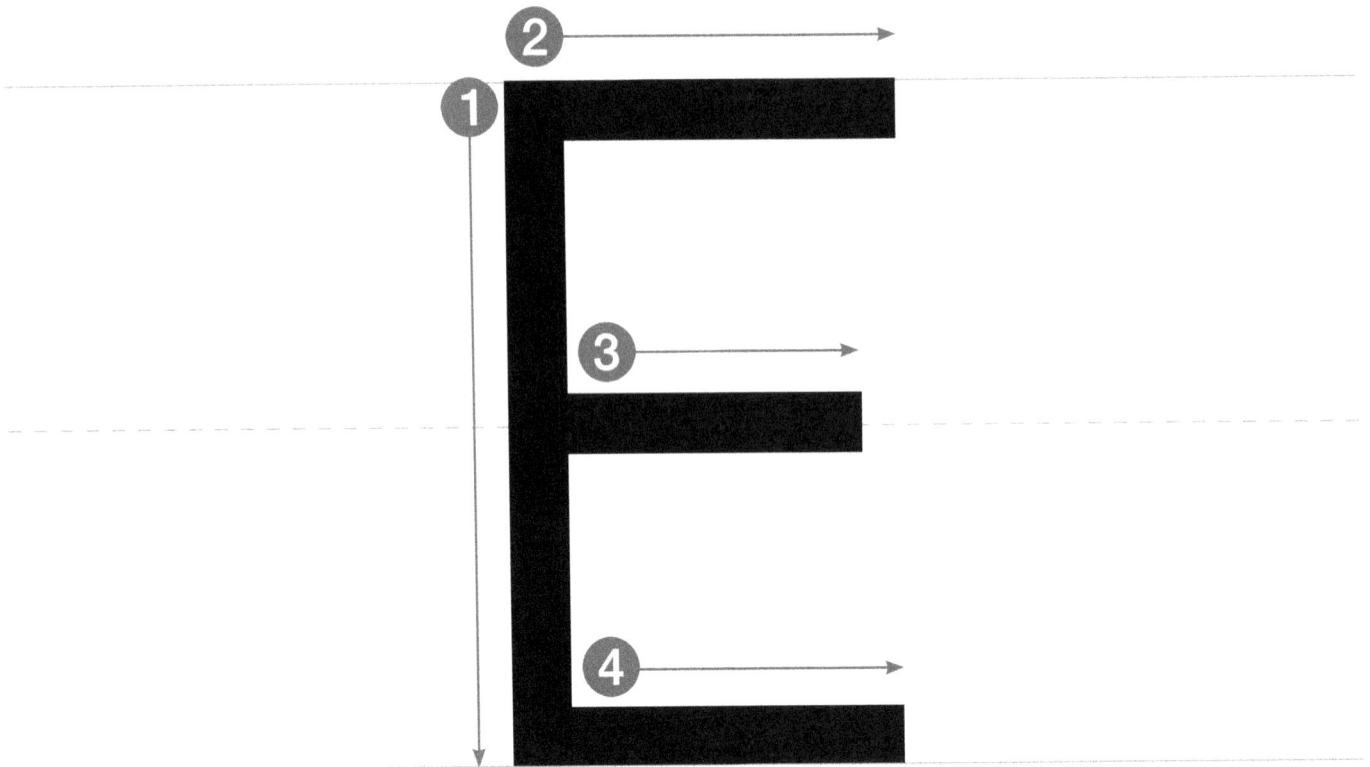

Directions:

1 Starting at the top go straight down.

Lift finger and bring back to the top.

2 Trace the top line.

Lift finger.

3 Trace the middle line.

Lift finger.

4 Trace the bottom line.

Say verbal clue when tracing E

"DOWN ... TRACE TOP ...

TRACE MIDDLE ... TRACE BOTTOM"

Have child say verbal clue as they trace the letter with their finger

"DOWN ... TRACE TOP ... TRACE MIDDLE ... TRACE BOTTOM"

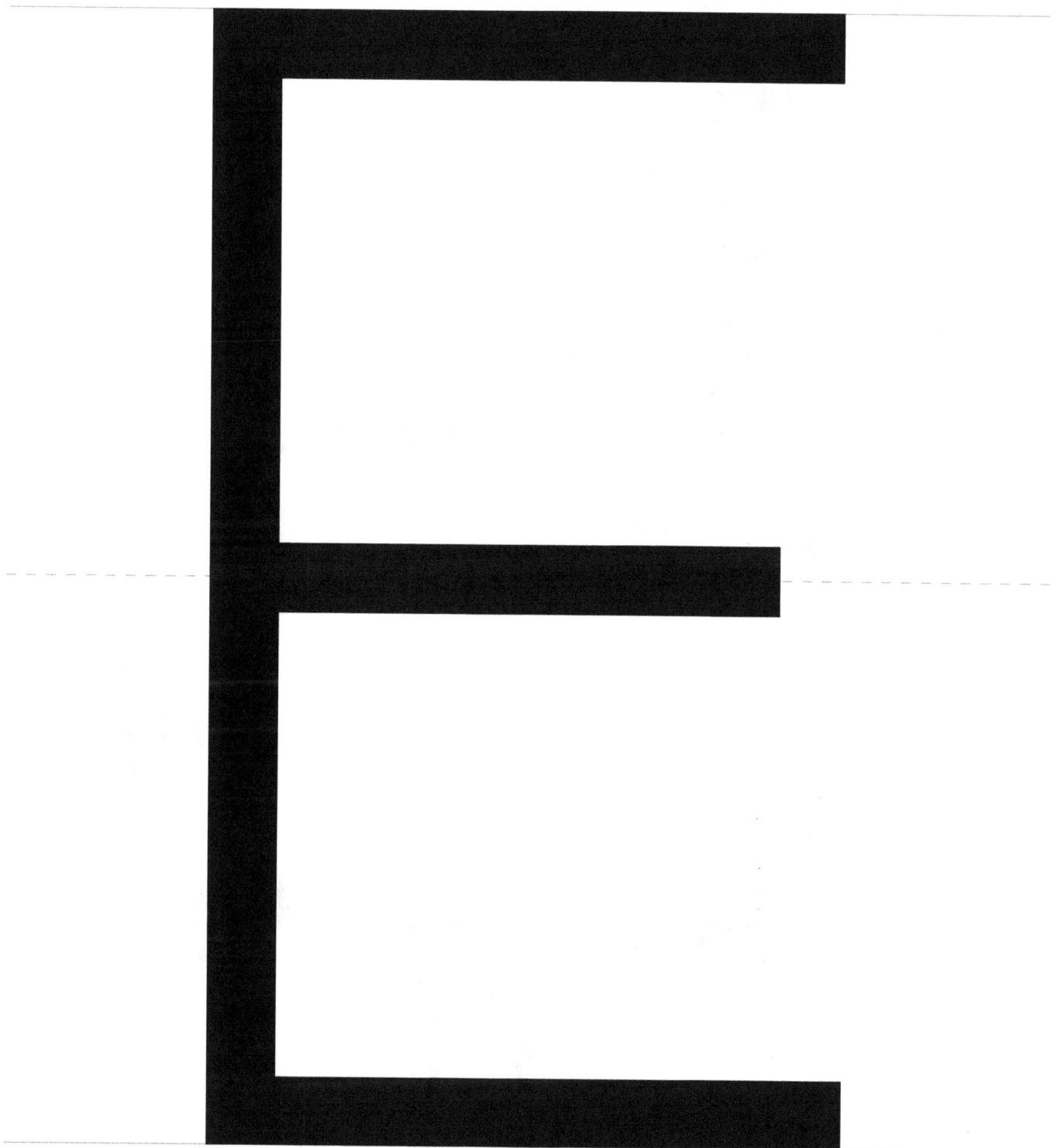

Trace the letters with a pencil.

Color the Emu.

Trace E and print your own letter E four times with a pencil.

Draw a picture that starts with E.

Demonstrate how to finger trace letter F.
Have child practice on the next page.

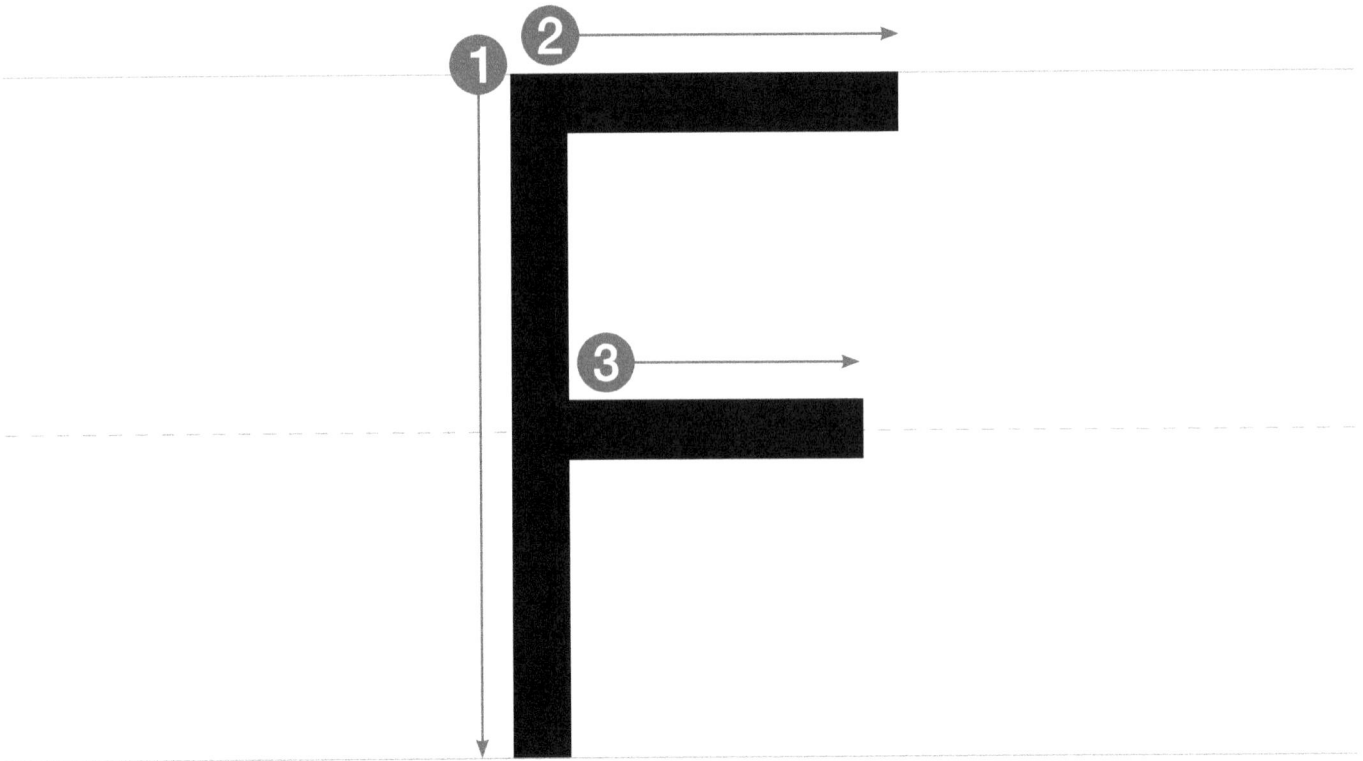

Directions:

1 Starting at the top go straight down.
Lift finger and bring back to the top.

2 Trace the top line.

3 Trace the middle line.

Say verbal clue when tracing F

**"DOWN ... TRACE TOP ...
TRACE MIDDLE"**

Have child say verbal clue as they trace the letter with their finger
"DOWN ... TRACE TOP ... TRACE MIDDLE"

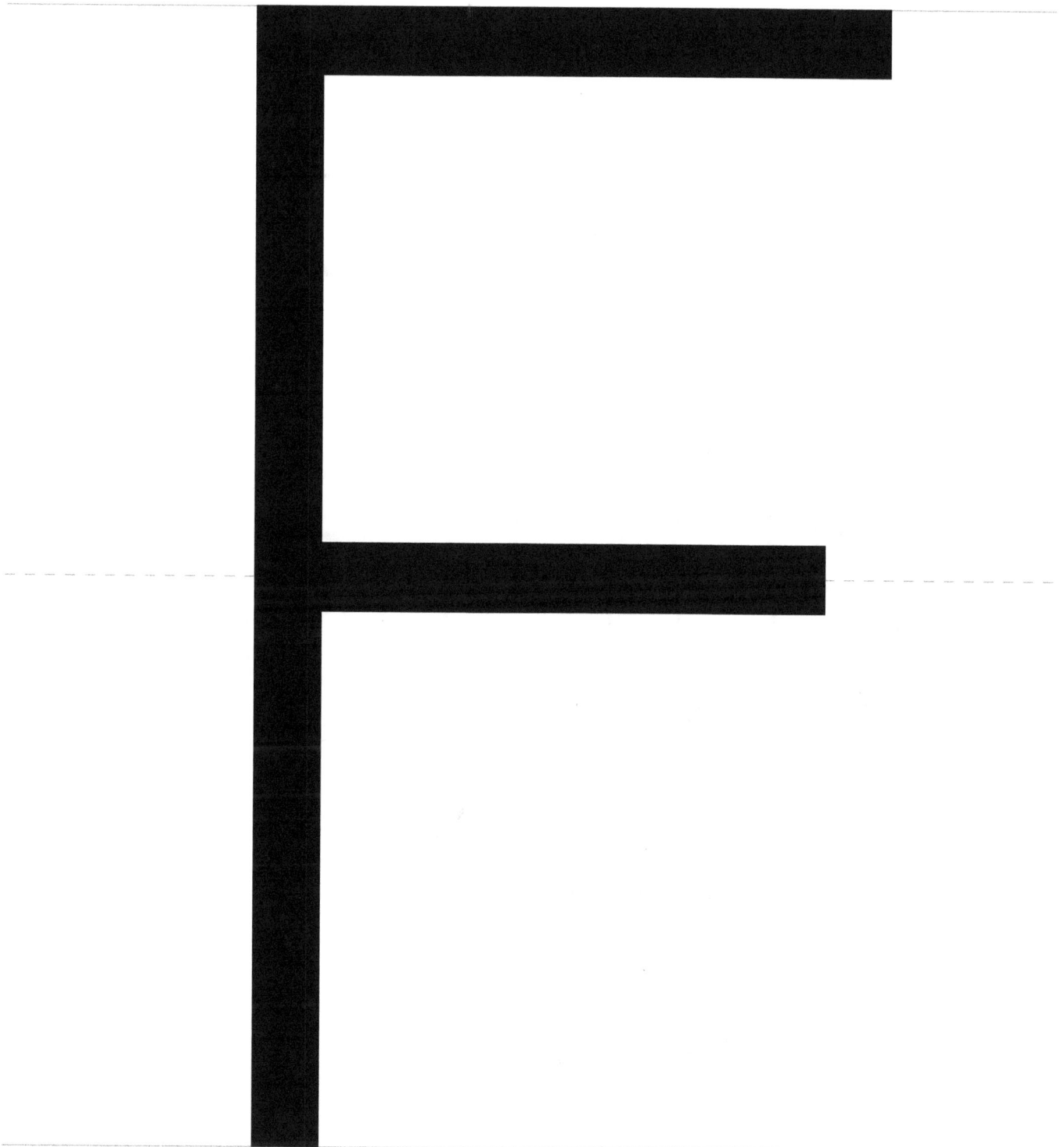

Trace the letters with a pencil.

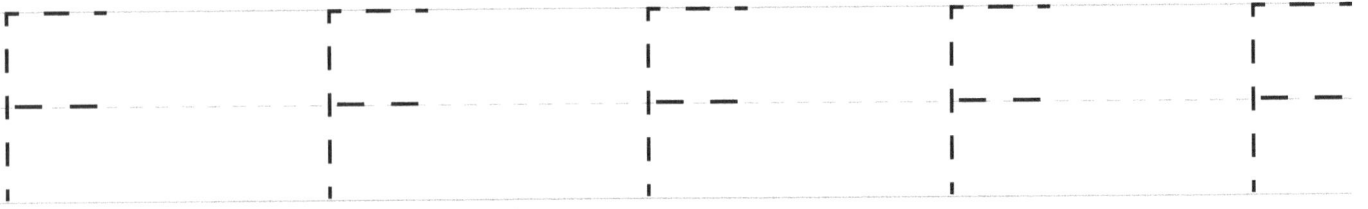

Color the Fish.

Trace F and print your own letter F four times with a pencil.

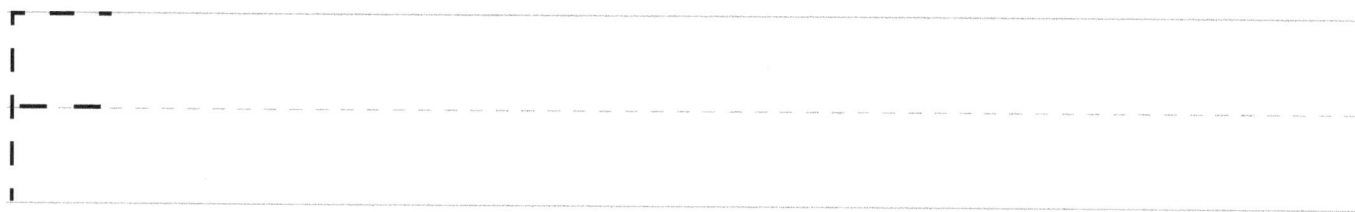

Draw a picture that starts with F.

Demonstrate how to finger trace letter G.
Have child practice on the next page.

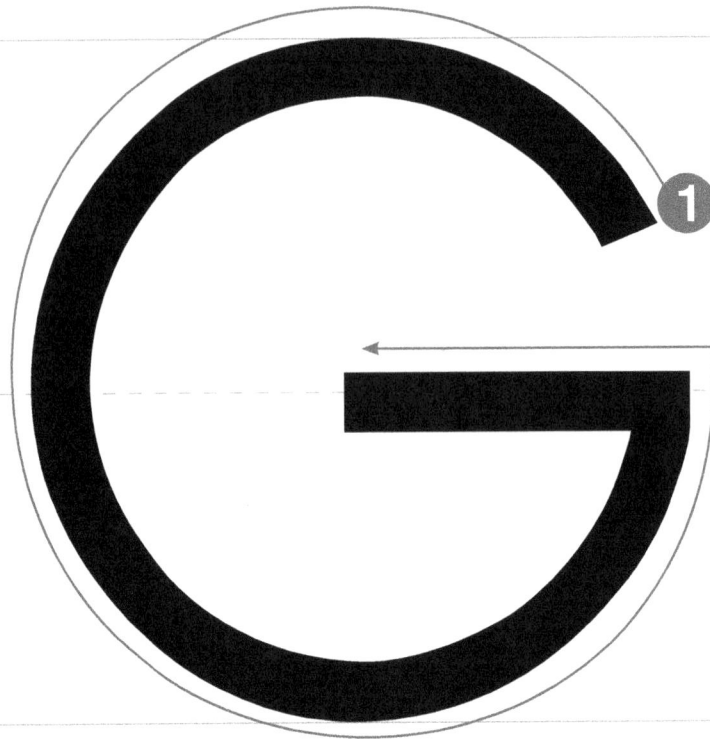

G ①

Directions:

① Starting below the top and without lifting your finger, circle left, up and around to middle then short line to left.

Say verbal clue when tracing G

"CIRCLE UP AND AROUND ... THEN IN"

Have child say verbal clue as they trace the letter with their finger

"CIRCLE UP AND AROUND ... THEN IN"

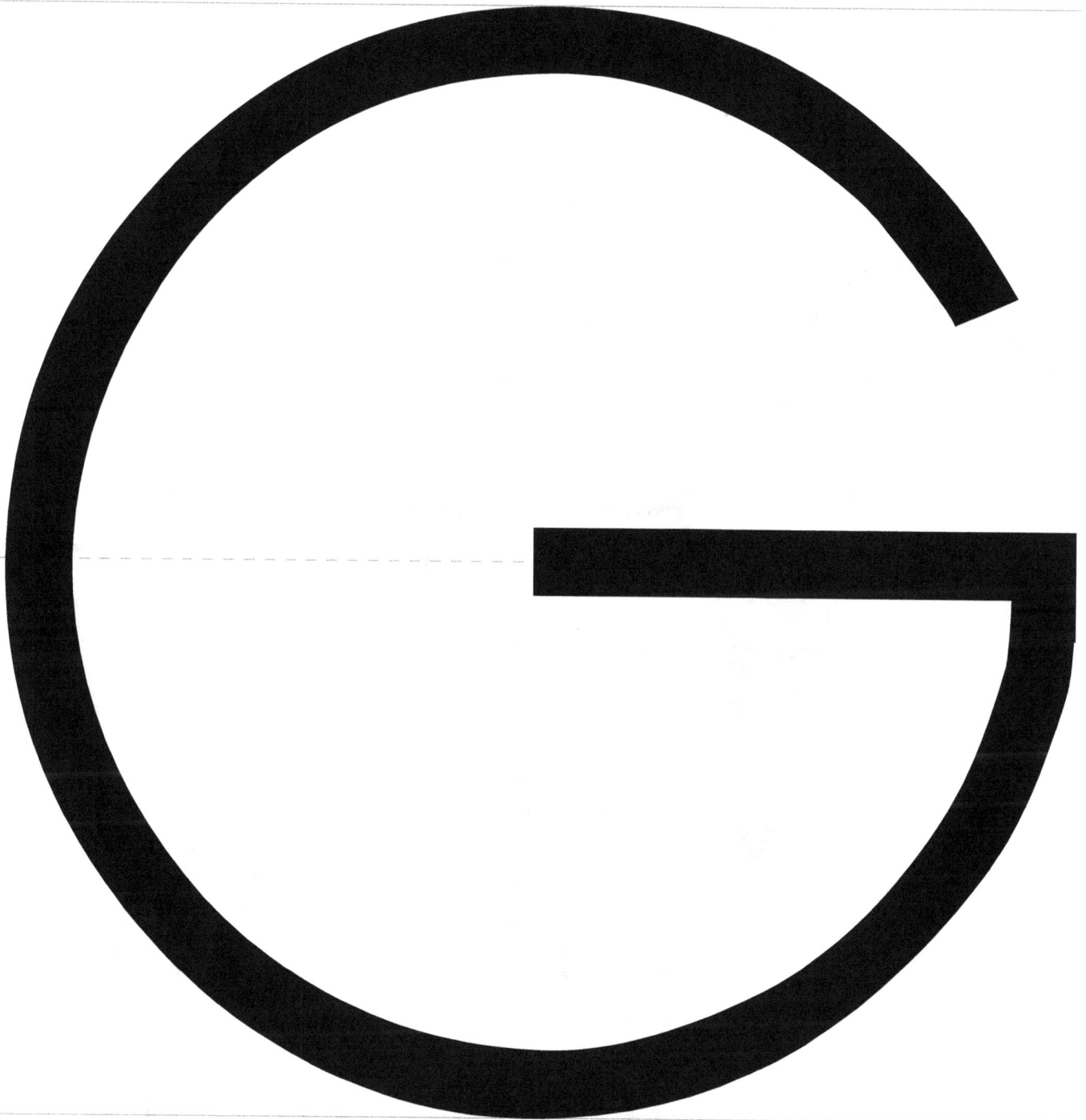

Trace the letters with a pencil.

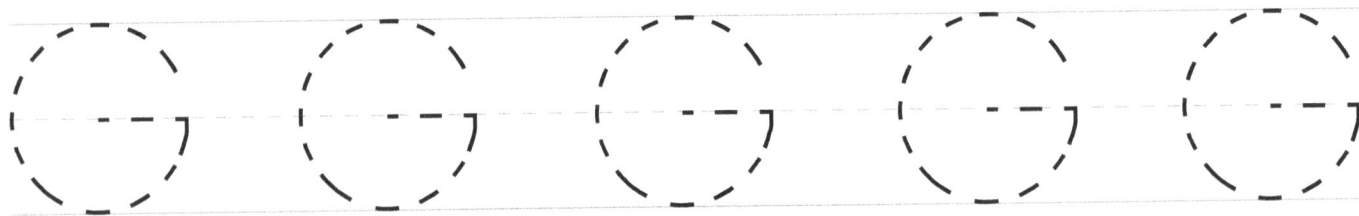

G G G G G

Color the Goat.

Trace G and print your own letter G four times with a pencil.

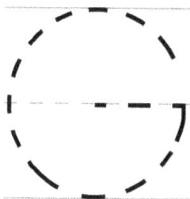

Draw a picture that starts with G.

Demonstrate how to finger trace letter H.
Have child practice on the next page.

Directions:

1 Starting at the top left go straight down.
Lift finger.

2 From the top right go straight down.

3 Connect the lines left to right on the middle line.

Say verbal clue when tracing H
"DOWN ... DOWN ... CONNECT"

Have child say verbal clue as they trace the letter with their finger
"DOWN ... DOWN ... CONNECT"

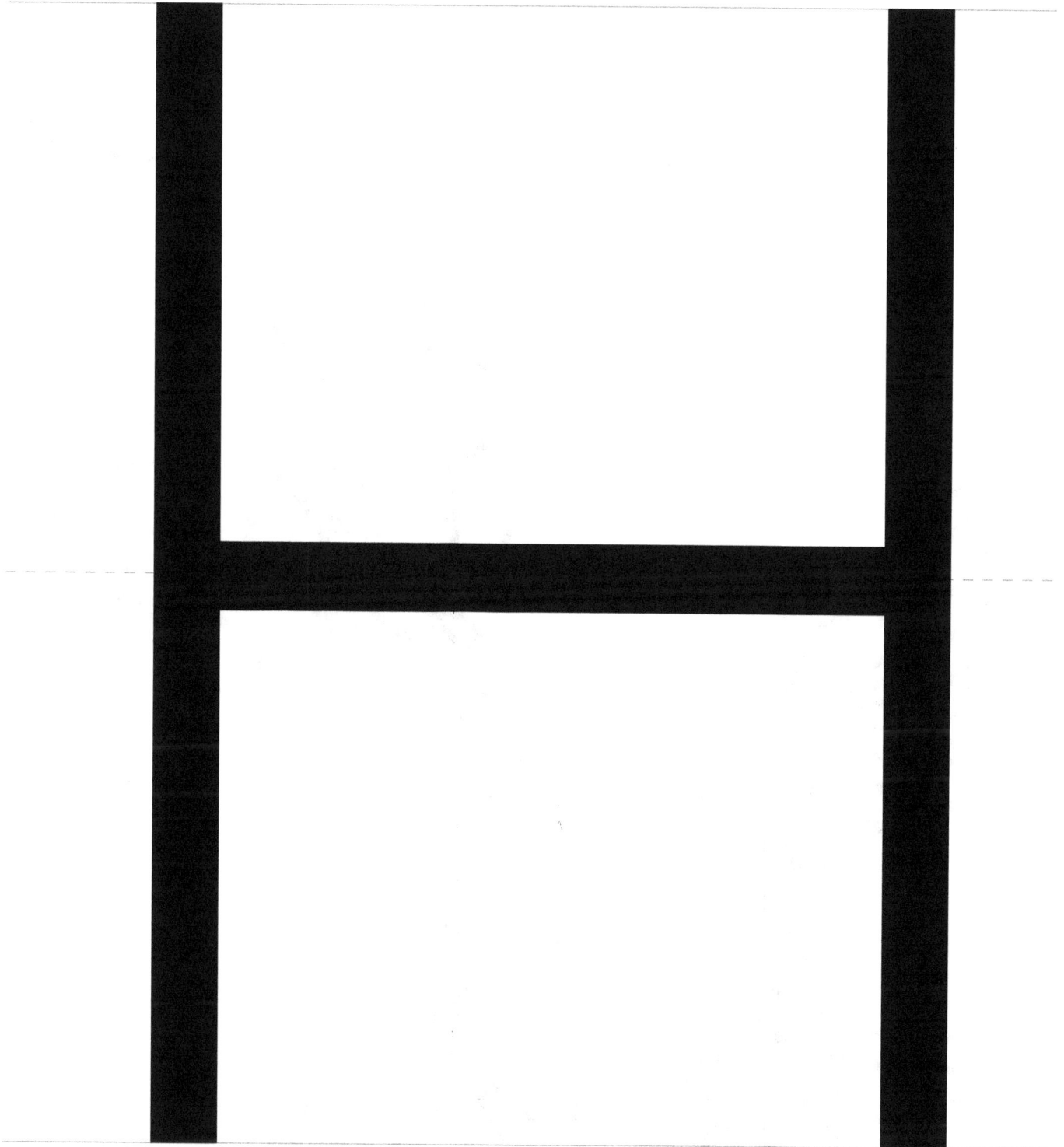

Trace the letters with a pencil.

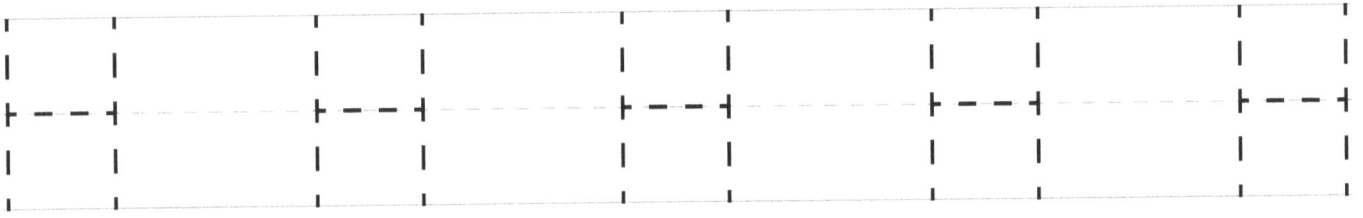

Color the Hummingbird.

Trace H and print your own letter H four times with a pencil.

Draw a picture that starts with H.

Demonstrate how to finger trace letter I.
Have child practice on the next page.

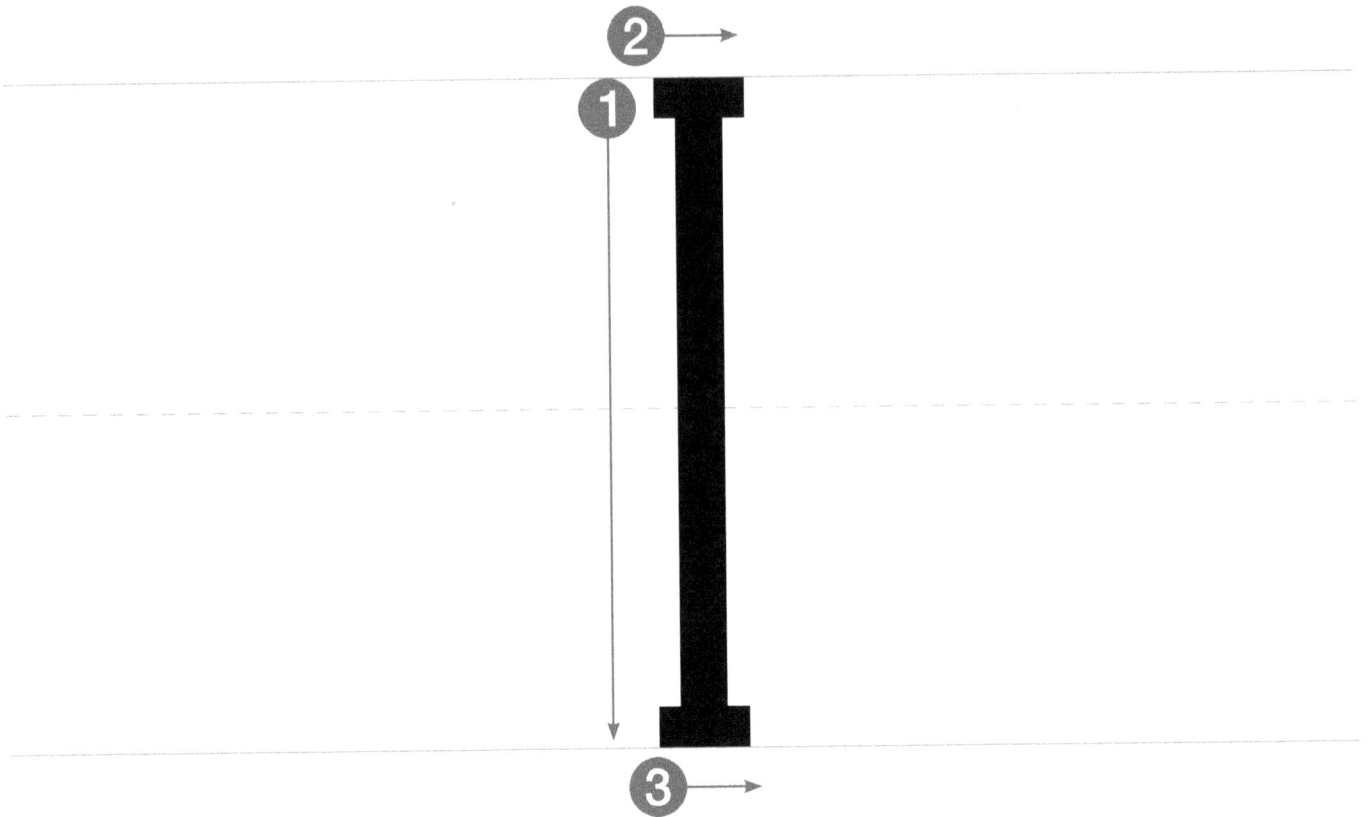

Directions:

1 Starting at the top go straight down.

 Lift finger.

2 Trace line at top left to right.

 Lift finger.

3 Trace line at bottom left to right.

Say verbal clue when tracing I
**"DOWN ... TRACE TOP ...
TRACE BOTTOM"**

Have child say verbal clue as they trace the letter with their finger
"DOWN ... TRACE TOP ... TRACE BOTTOM"

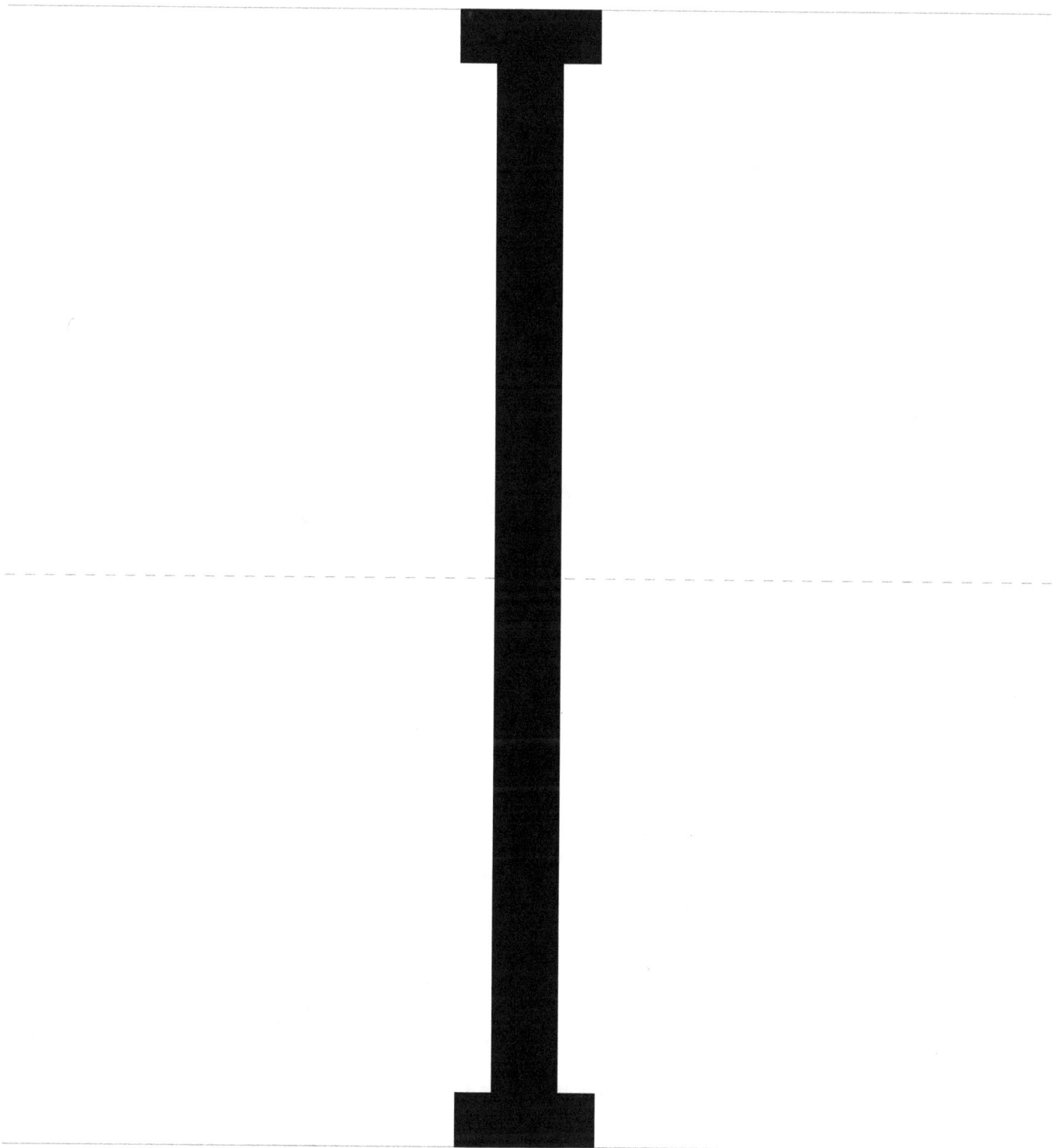

I

Trace the letters with a pencil.

Color the Iguana.

Trace I and print your own letter I four times with a pencil.

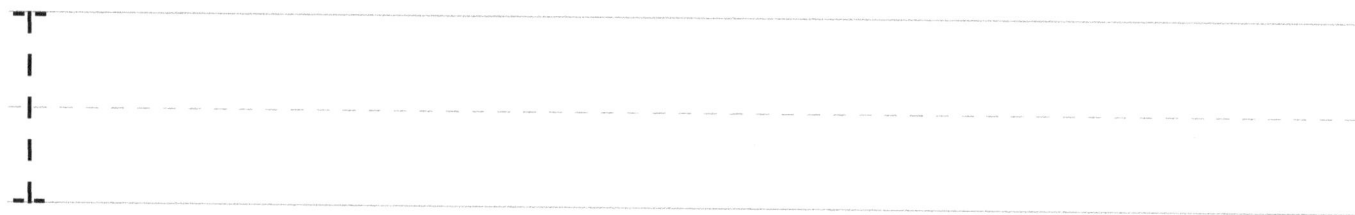

Draw a picture that starts with I.

Demonstrate how to finger trace letter J.
Have child practice on the next page.

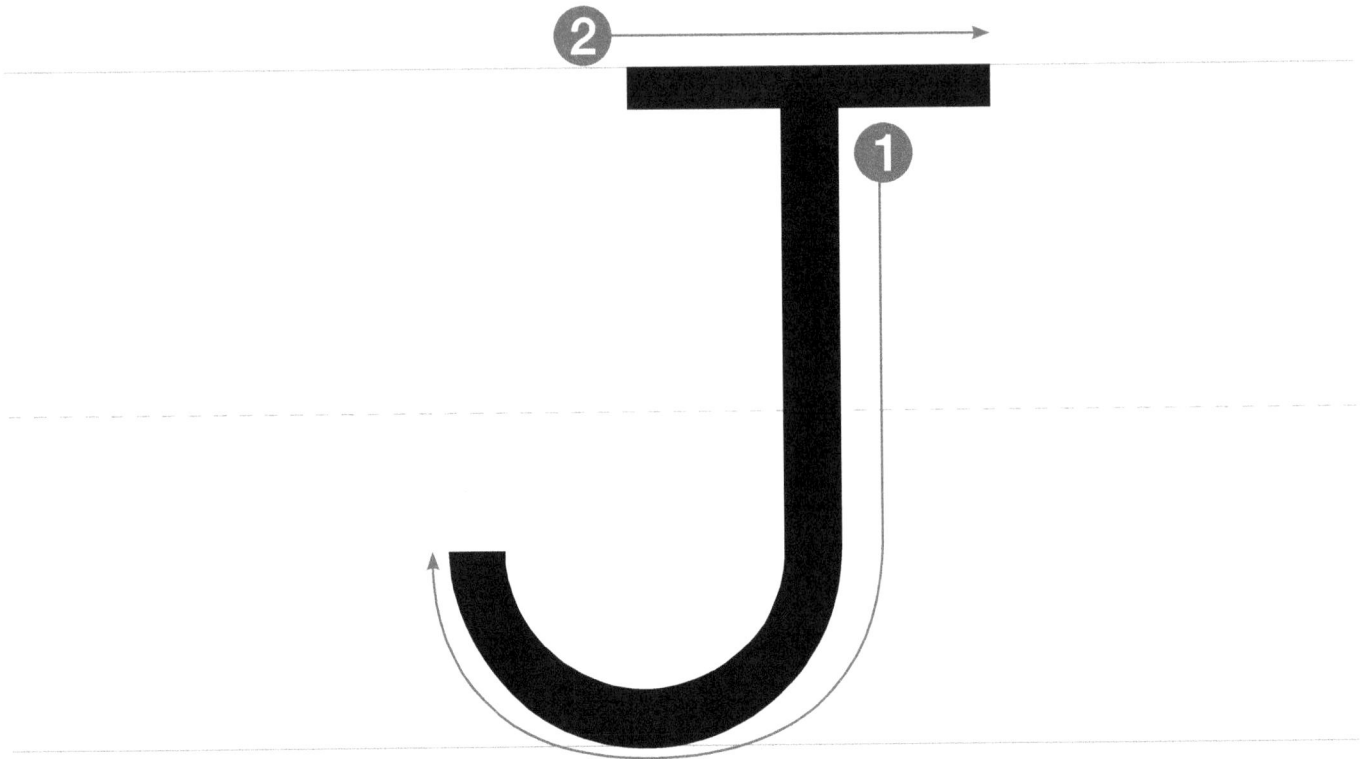

② →

J

①

Directions:

① Starting at the top go straight
down and curve left.

Lift finger.

② Trace line at top left to right.

Say verbal clue when tracing J

**"DOWN ... CURVE ...
TRACE TOP"**

Have child say verbal clue as they trace the letter with their finger
"DOWN ... CURVE ... TRACE TOP"

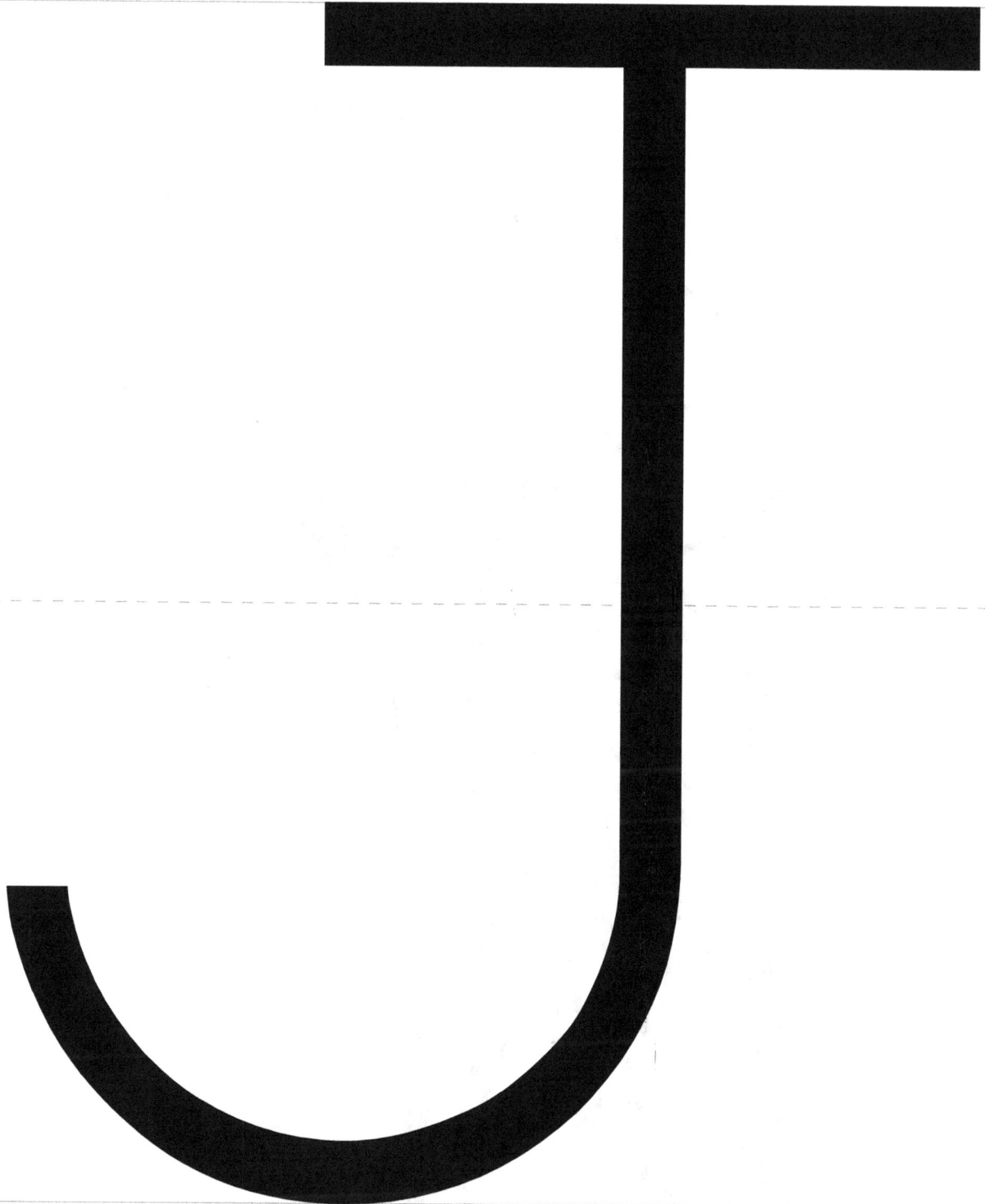

J

Trace the letters with a pencil.

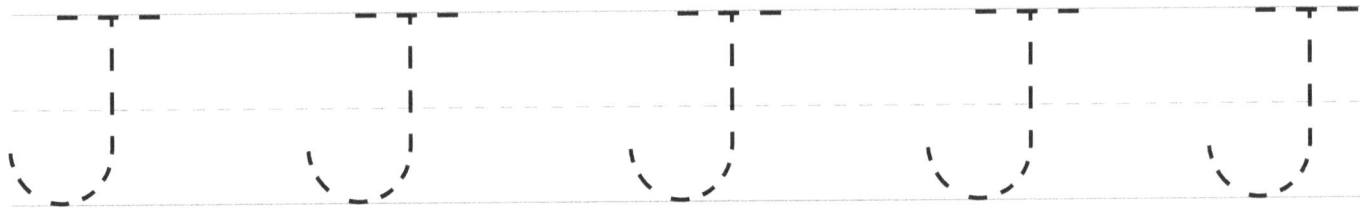

J J J J J

Color the Jellyfish.

Trace J and print your own letter J four times with a pencil.

J

Draw a picture that starts with J.

Demonstrate how to finger trace letter K.
Have child practice on the next page.

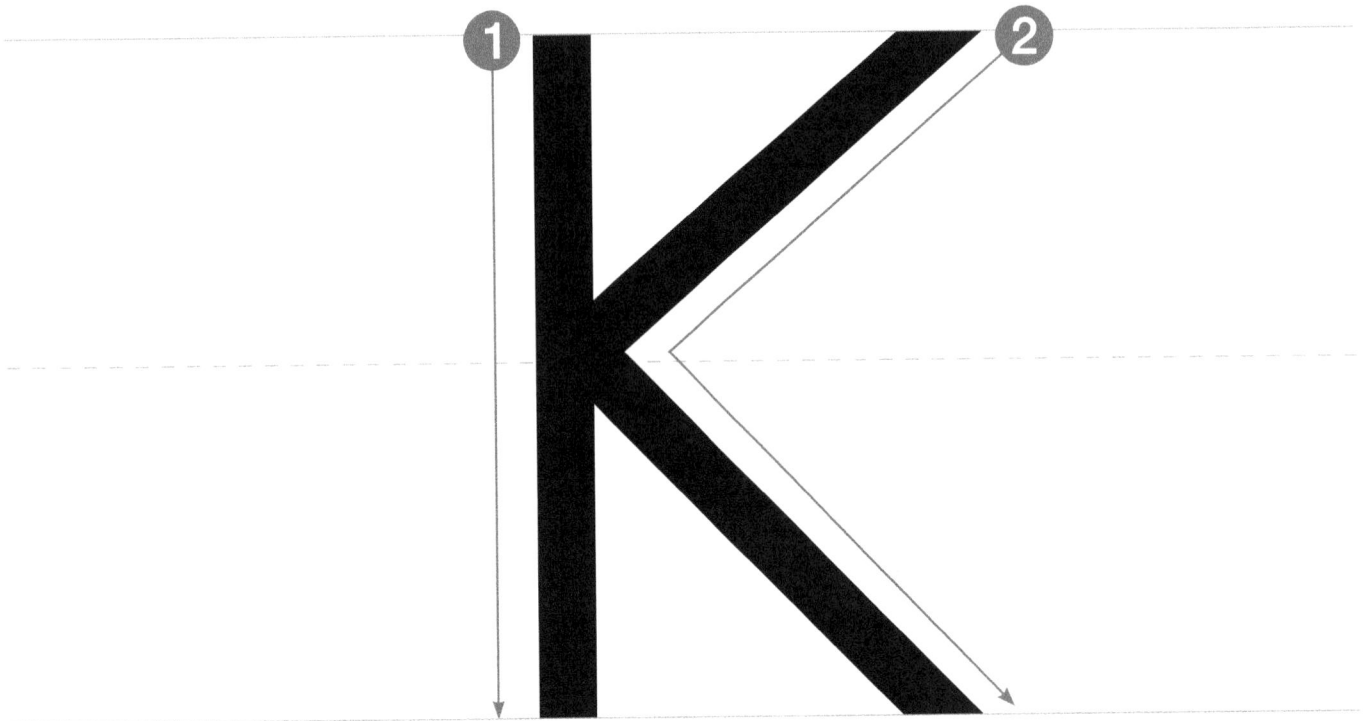

Directions:

1 Starting at the top go straight down.
Lift finger and bring back to the top.

2 Slant second line to the middle
then slant to the bottom without
lifting your finger.

Say verbal clue when tracing K

"DOWN ... SLANT IN ... SLANT OUT"

Have child say verbal clue as they trace the letter with their finger
"DOWN ... SLANT IN ... SLANT OUT"

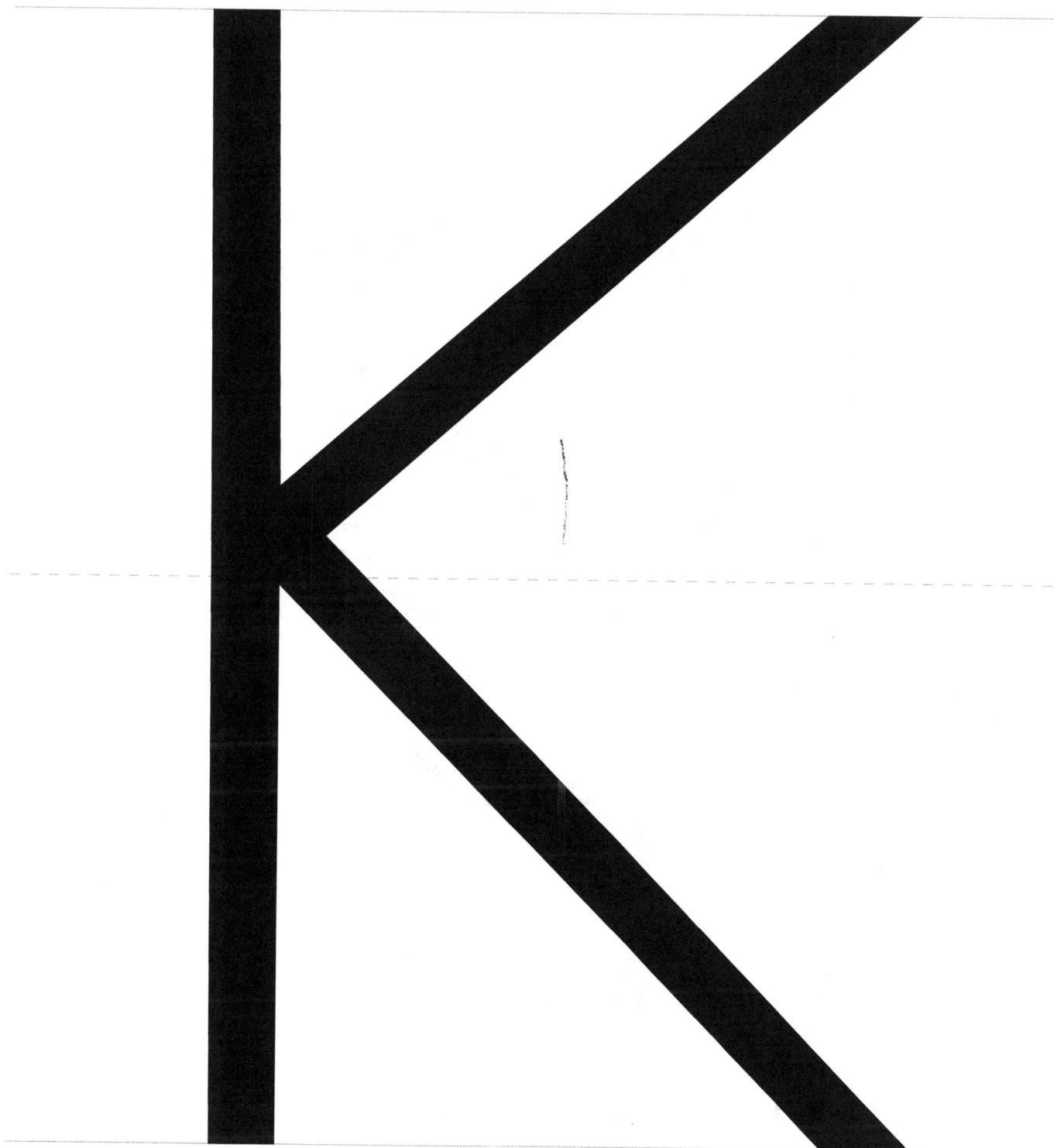

Trace the letters with a pencil.

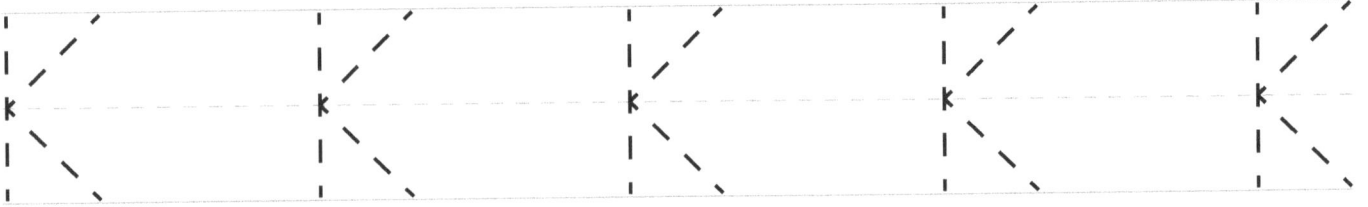

K K K K K

Color the Koala.

Trace K and print your own letter K four times with a pencil.

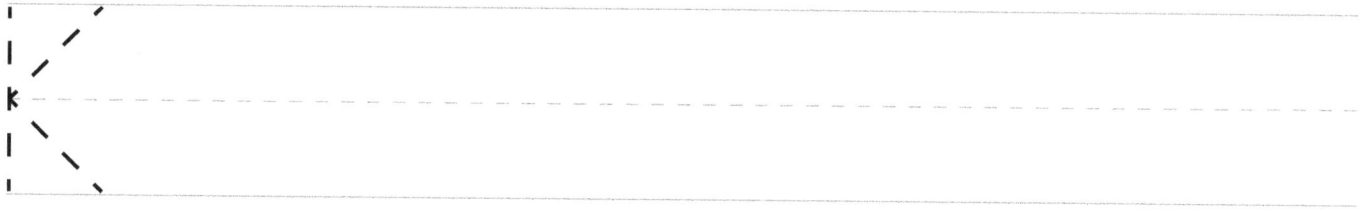

K

Draw a picture that starts with K.

Demonstrate how to finger trace letter L.
Have child practice on the next page.

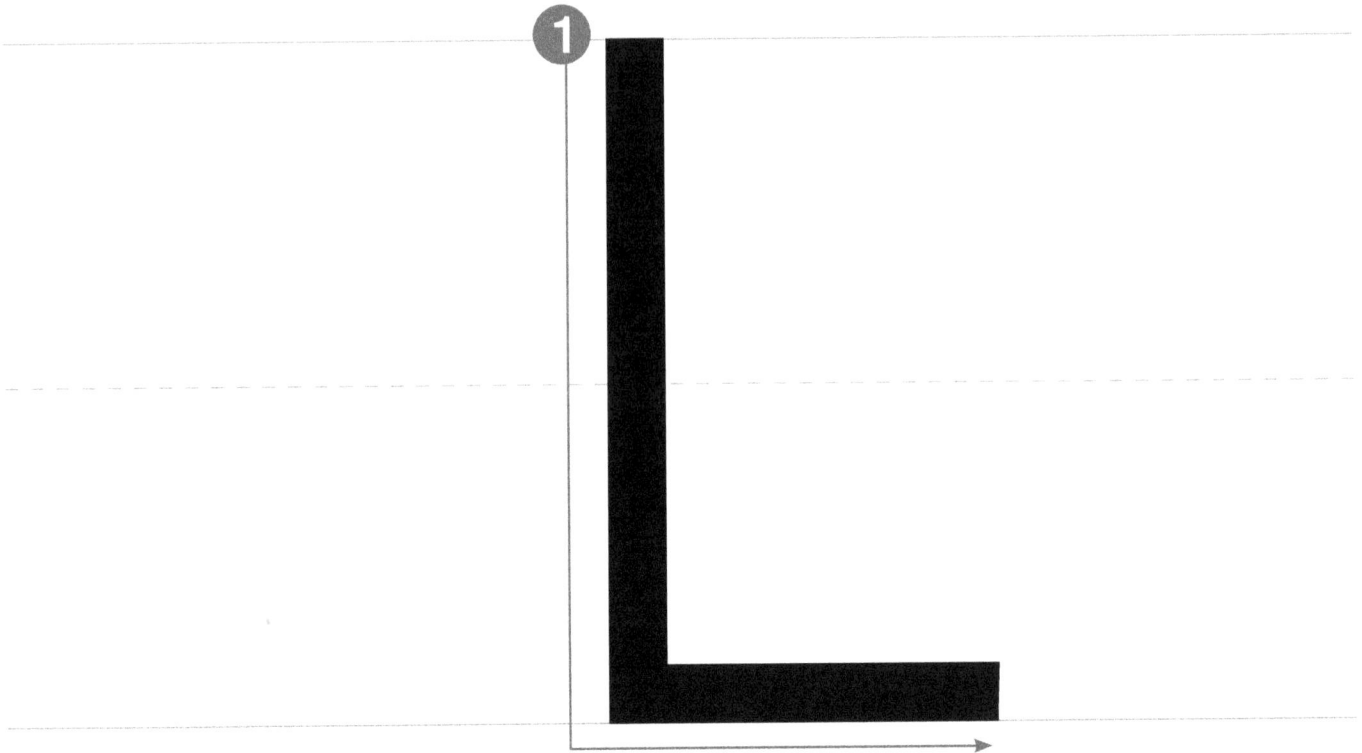

1

Directions:

1 Starting at the top and without lifting your finger go straight down and trace the bottom line to right.

Say verbal clue when tracing L
"DOWN ... TRACE BOTTOM"

Have child say verbal clue as they trace the letter with their finger

"DOWN ... TRACE BOTTOM"

L

Trace the letters with a pencil.

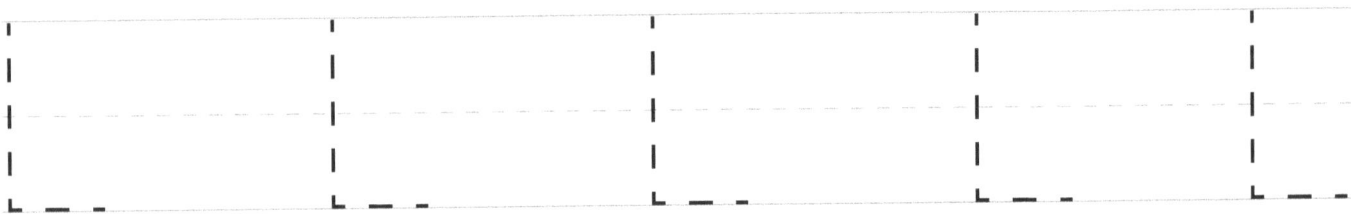

Color the Lobster.

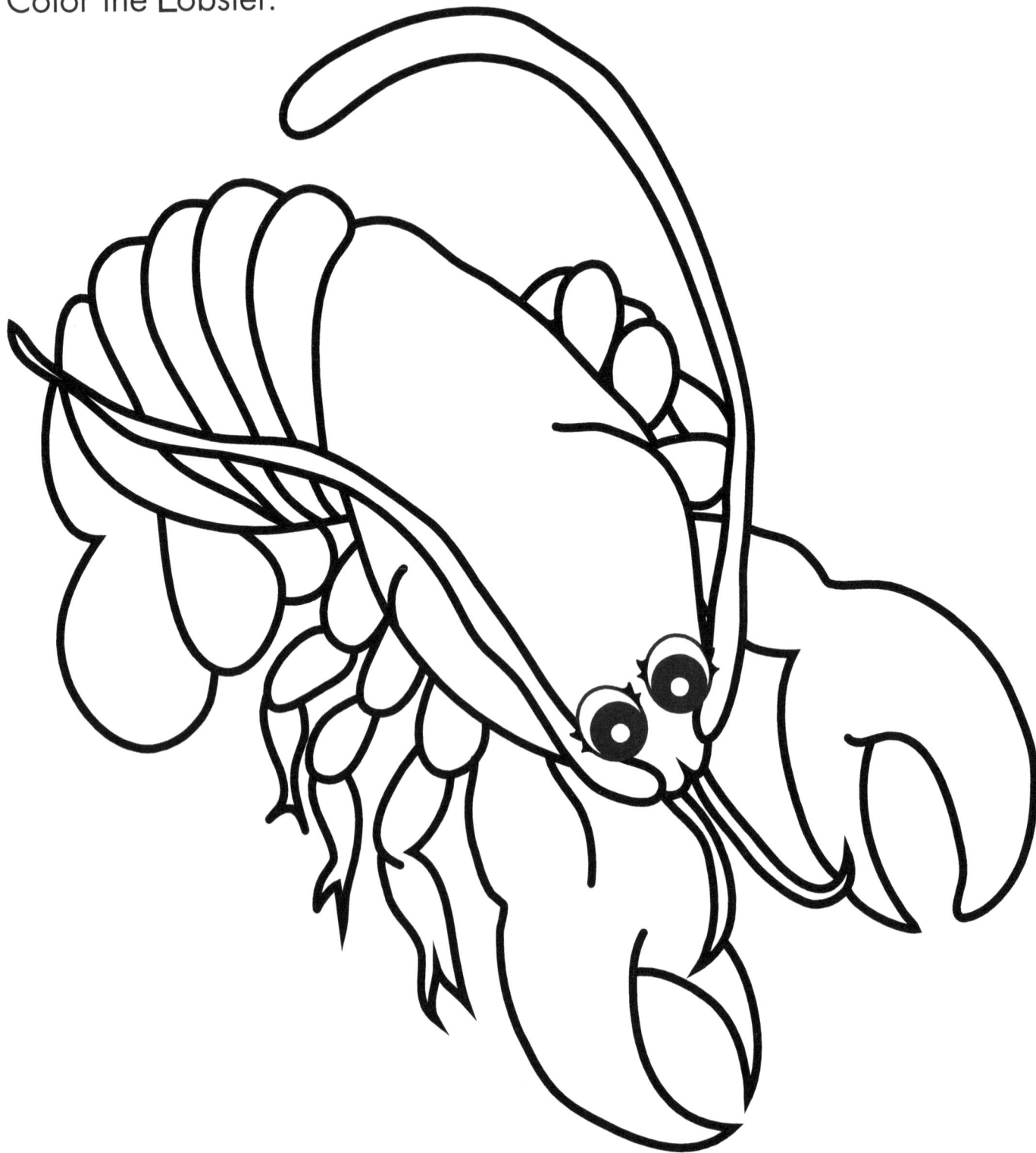

Trace L and print your own letter L four times with a pencil.

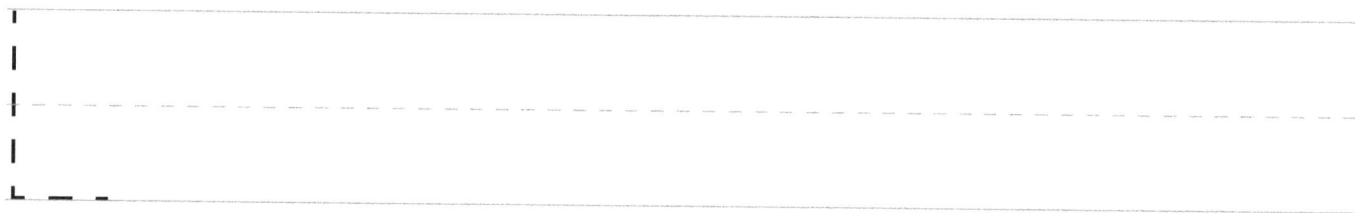

Draw a picture that starts with L.

Demonstrate how to finger trace letter M.
Have child practice on the next page.

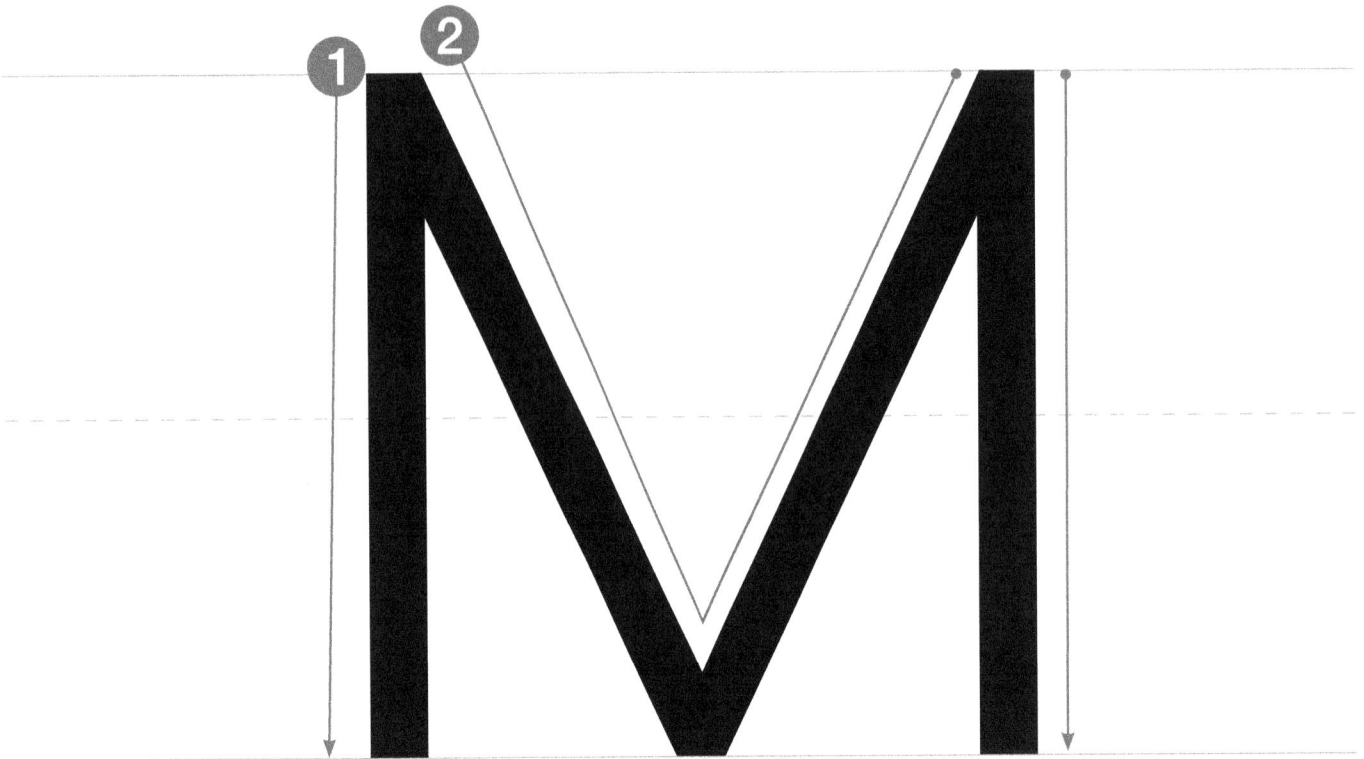

Directions:

1 Starting at the top go straight down.
Lift finger and bring back to the top.

2 Slant second line down to bottom, slant up to top and straight down without lifting your finger.

Say verbal clue when tracing M
**"DOWN ... SLANT DOWN ...
SLANT UP ... STRAIGHT DOWN"**

Have child say verbal clue as they trace the letter with their finger
**"DOWN ... SLANT DOWN ... SLANT UP
... STRAIGHT DOWN"**

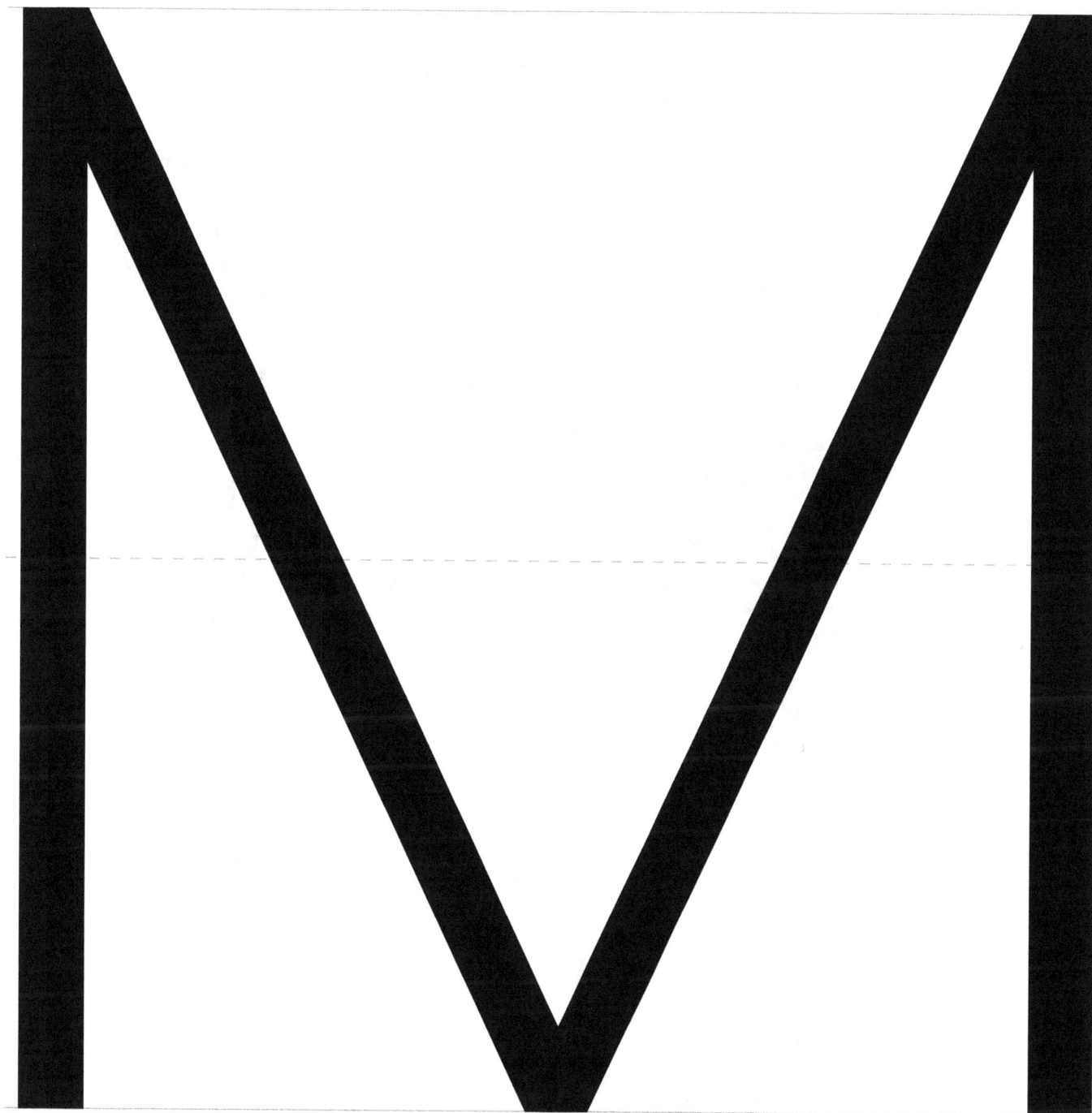

Trace the letters with a pencil.

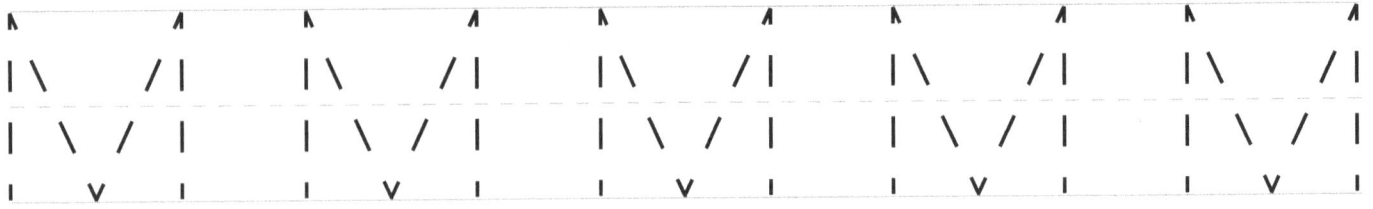

Color the Mouse.

Trace **M** and print your own letter **M** four times with a pencil.

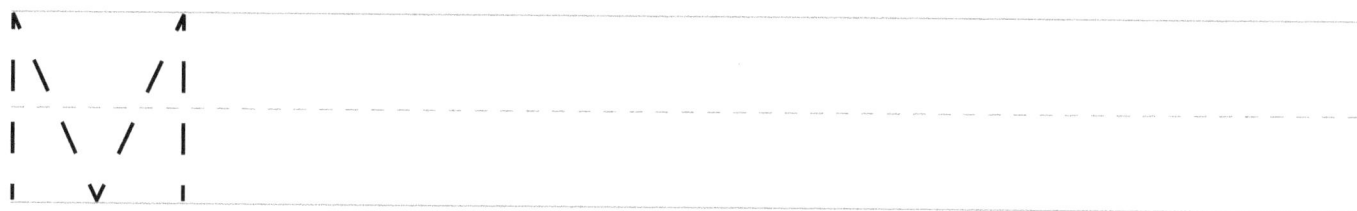

```
Λ     Λ
I \   / I
I  \ /  I
I   v   I
```

Draw a picture that starts with **M**.

Demonstrate how to finger trace letter N.
Have child practice on the next page.

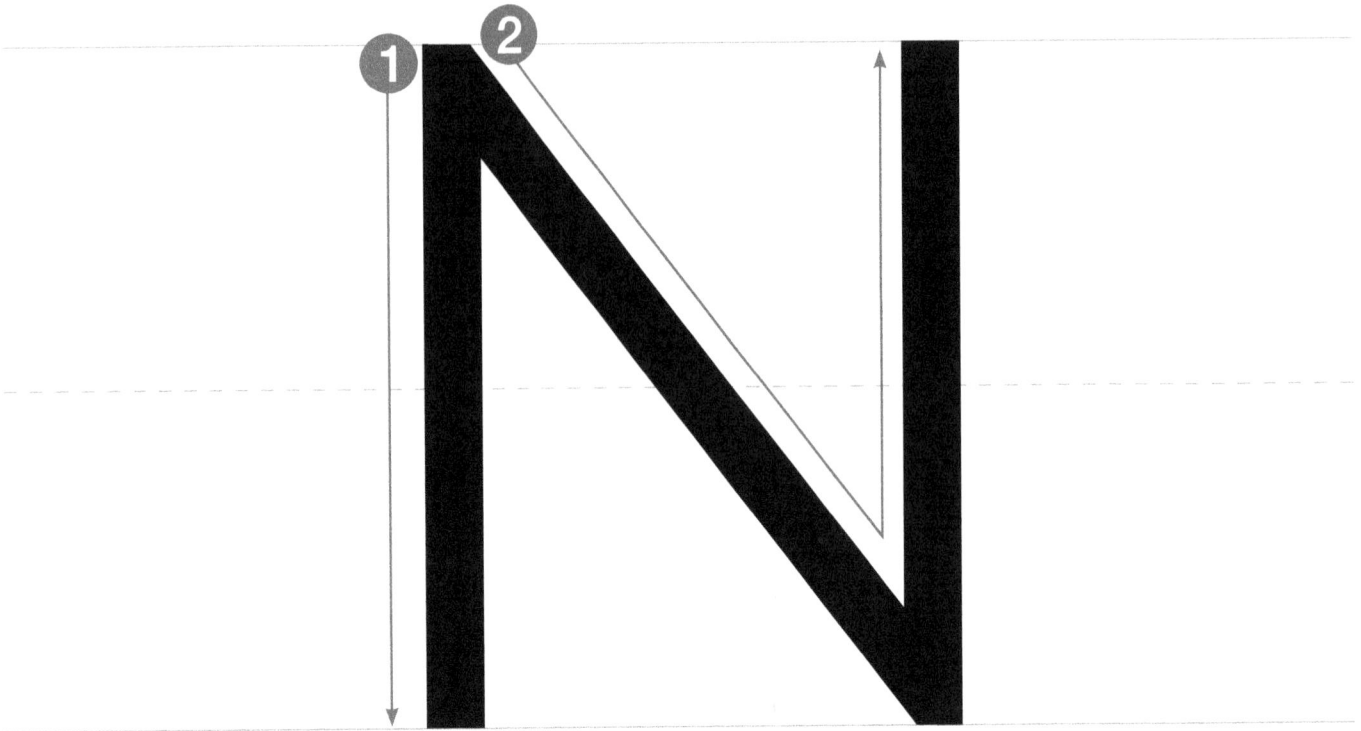

N

Directions:

1. Starting at the top go straight down.
   Lift finger and bring back to the top.

2. Slant second line to bottom and straight to top without lifting your finger.

Say verbal clue when tracing N

**"STRAIGHT DOWN ... SLANT DOWN ...
STRAIGHT UP"**

Have child say verbal clue as they trace the letter with their finger
"STRAIGHT DOWN ... SLANT DOWN ... STRAIGHT UP"

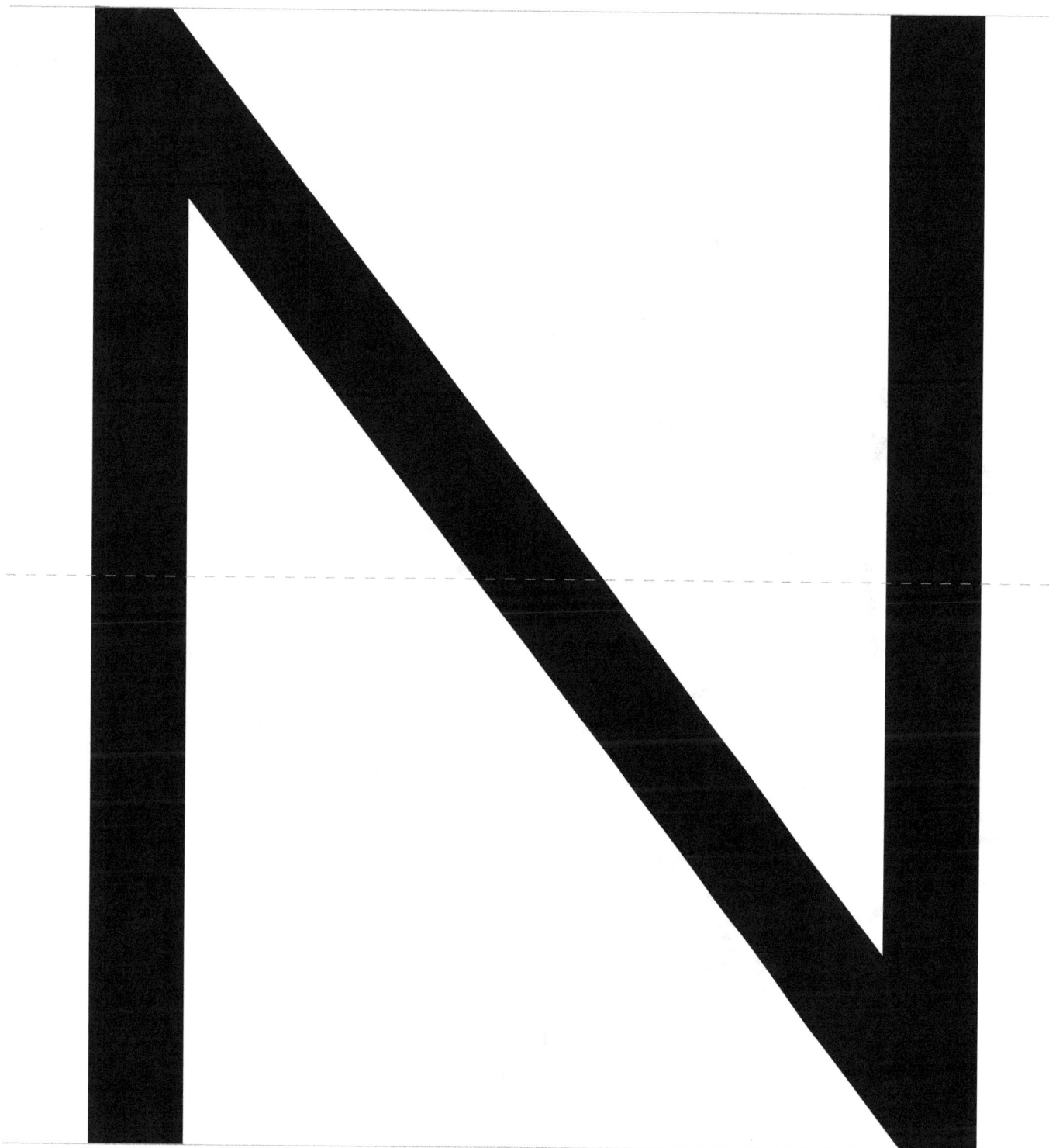

Trace the letters with a pencil.

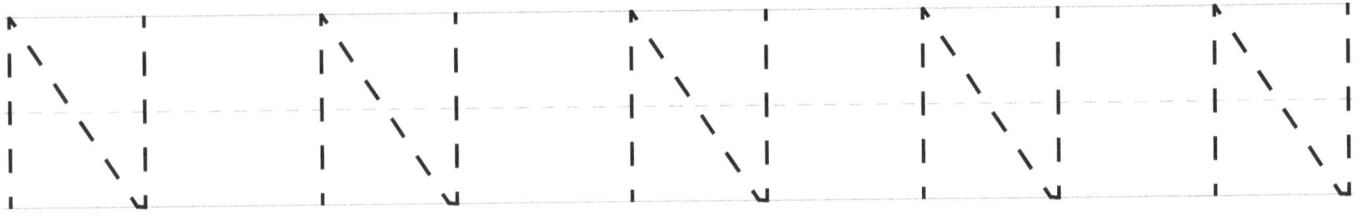

N N N N N

Color the Nightingale.

Trace **N** and print your own letter **N** four times with a pencil.

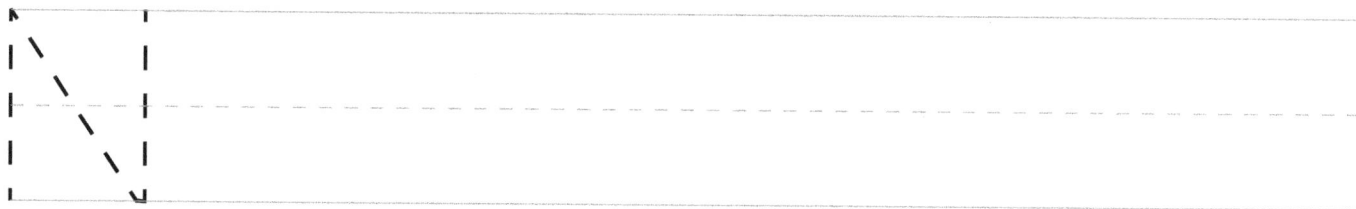

N

Draw a picture that starts with **N**.

Demonstrate how to finger trace letter O.
Have child practice on the next page.

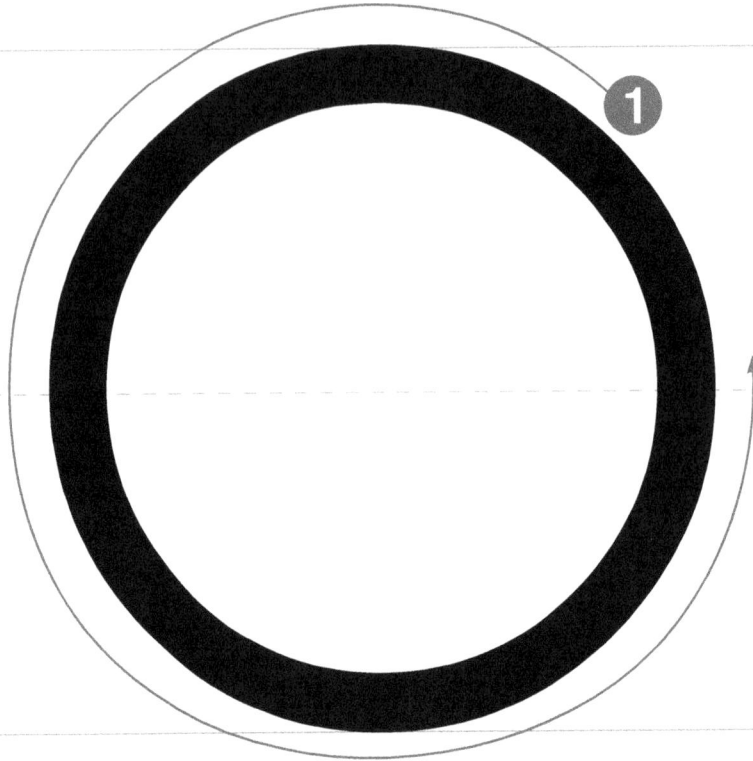

①

Directions:
① Starting below the top and without lifting
   your finger, circle left, up and around to close.

Say verbal clue when tracing O
"CIRCLE UP AND AROUND TO CLOSE"

Have child say verbal clue as they trace the letter with their finger

"CIRCLE UP AND AROUND TO CLOSE"

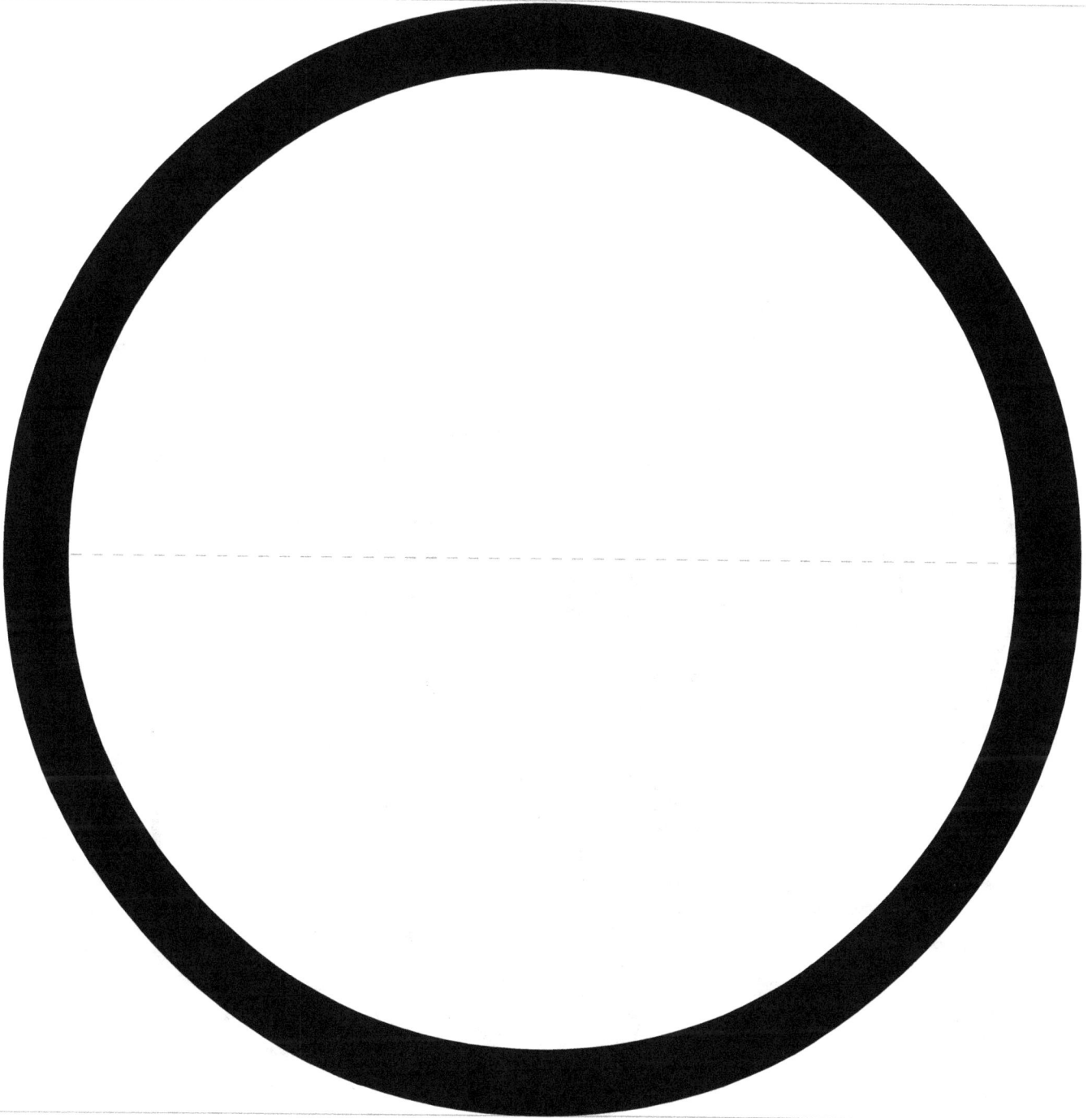

Trace the letters with a pencil.

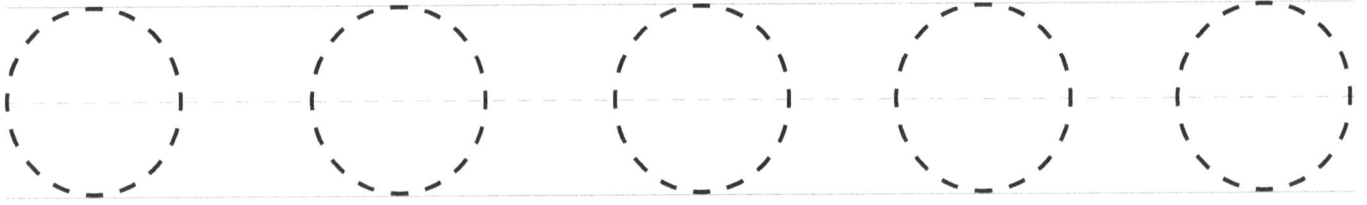

Color the Octopus.

Trace O and print your own letter O four times with a pencil.

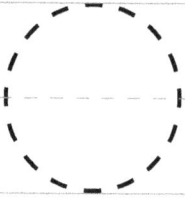

Draw a picture that starts with O.

Demonstrate how to finger trace letter P.
Have child practice on the next page.

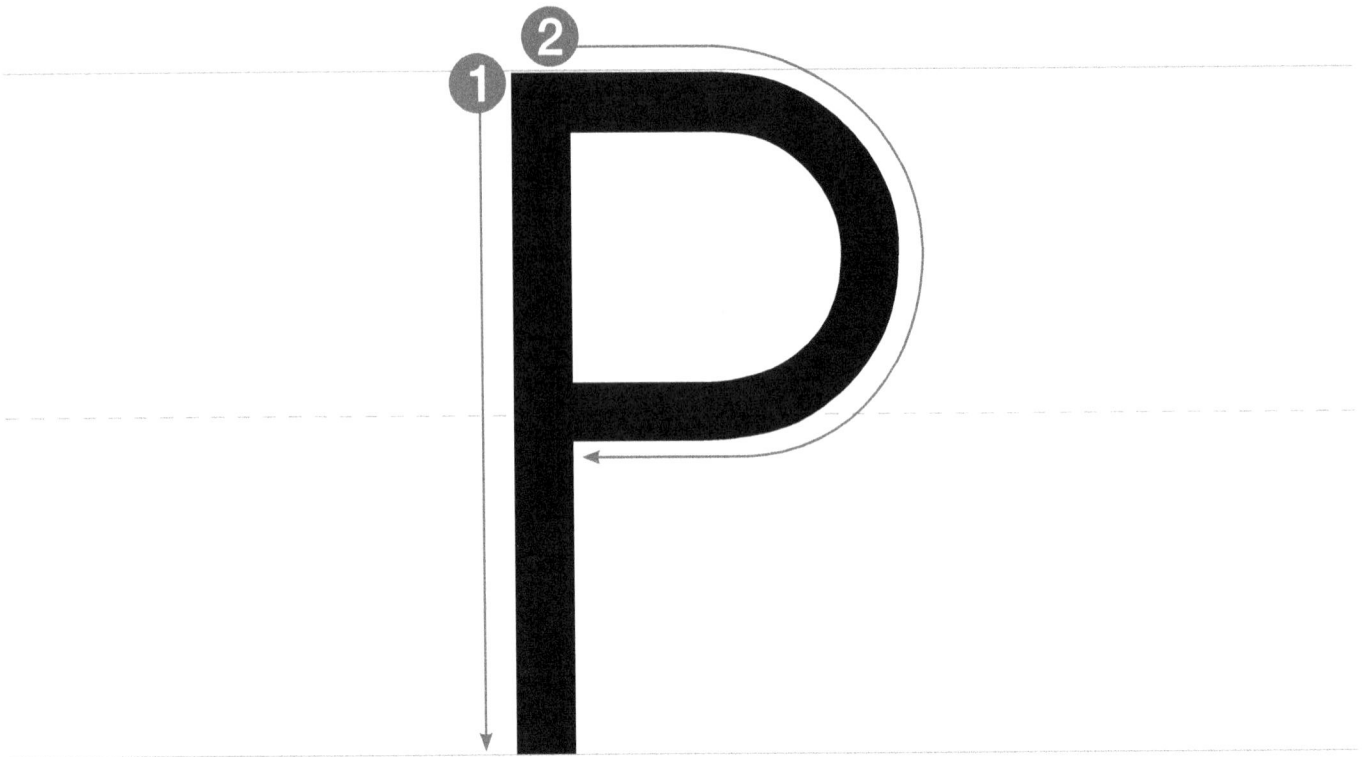

Directions:

1 Starting at the top go straight down.
   Lift finger and bring back to the top.

2 Curve around to the middle.

Say verbal clue when tracing P

"DOWN ... BACK TO THE TOP ...
AROUND TO MIDDLE"

Have child say verbal clue as they trace the letter with their finger
"DOWN ... BACK TO THE TOP ... AROUND TO MIDDLE"

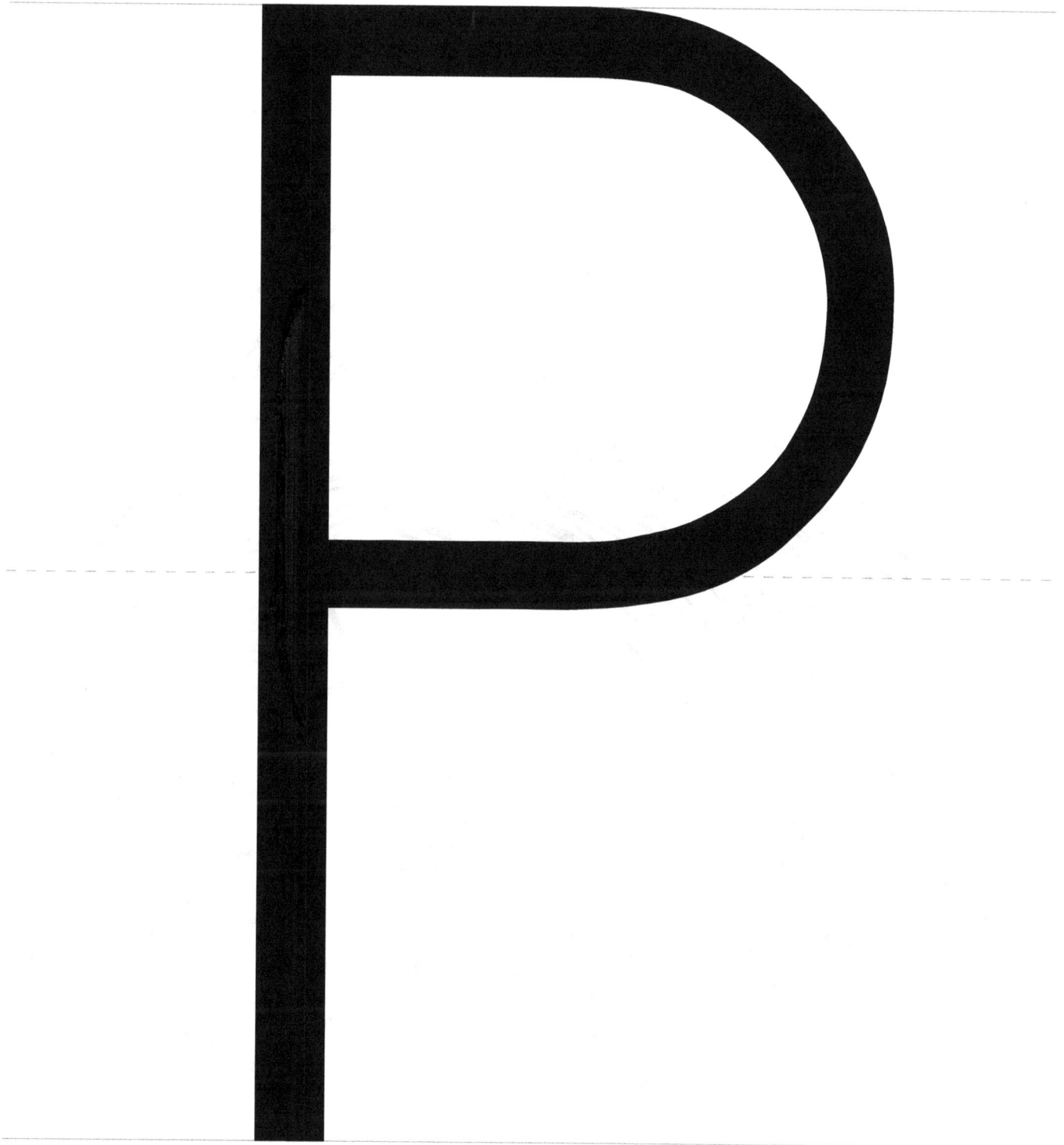

Trace the letters with a pencil.

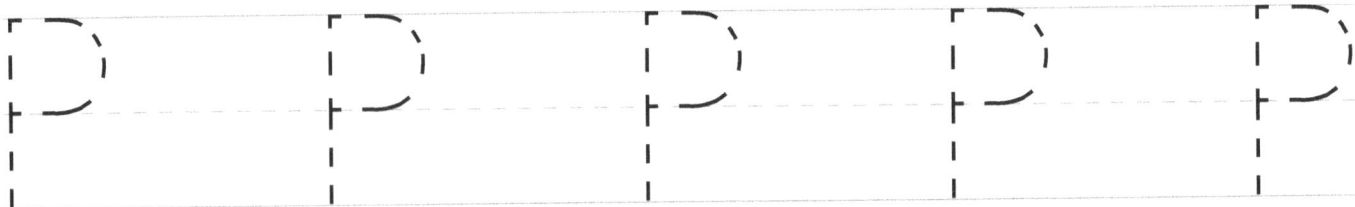

P P P P P

Color the Porcupine.

Trace P and print your own letter P four times with a pencil.

P

Draw a picture that starts with P.

Demonstrate how to finger trace letter Q.
Have child practice on the next page.

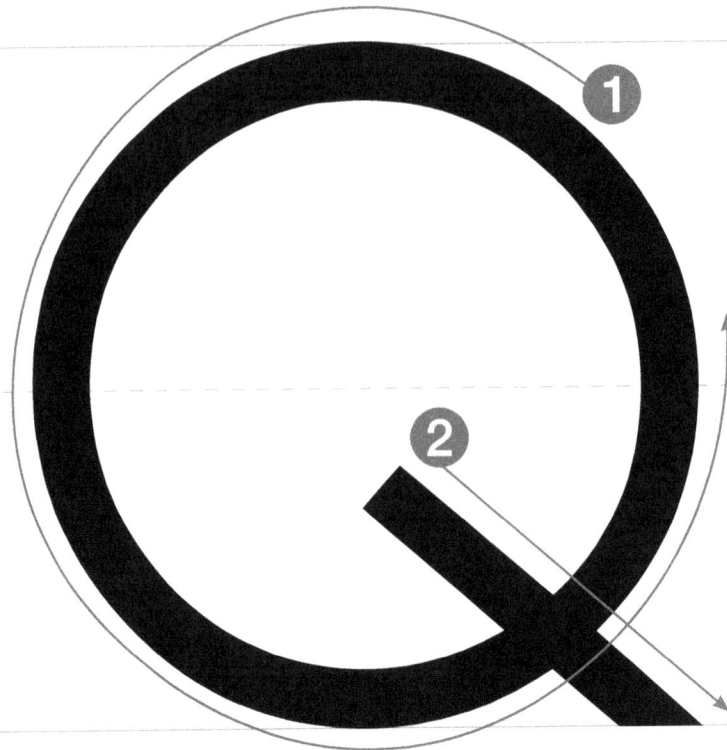

Directions:

1 Starting below the top and without
lifting your finger, circle left, up and
around to close.

Lift finger.

2 Add right slanted line at bottom.

Say verbal clue when tracing Q

**"CIRCLE UP AND AROUND TO CLOSE ...
ADD SLANTED LINE"**

Have child say verbal clue as they trace the letter with their finger

"CIRCLE UP AND AROUND TO CLOSE ...
ADD SLANTED LINE"

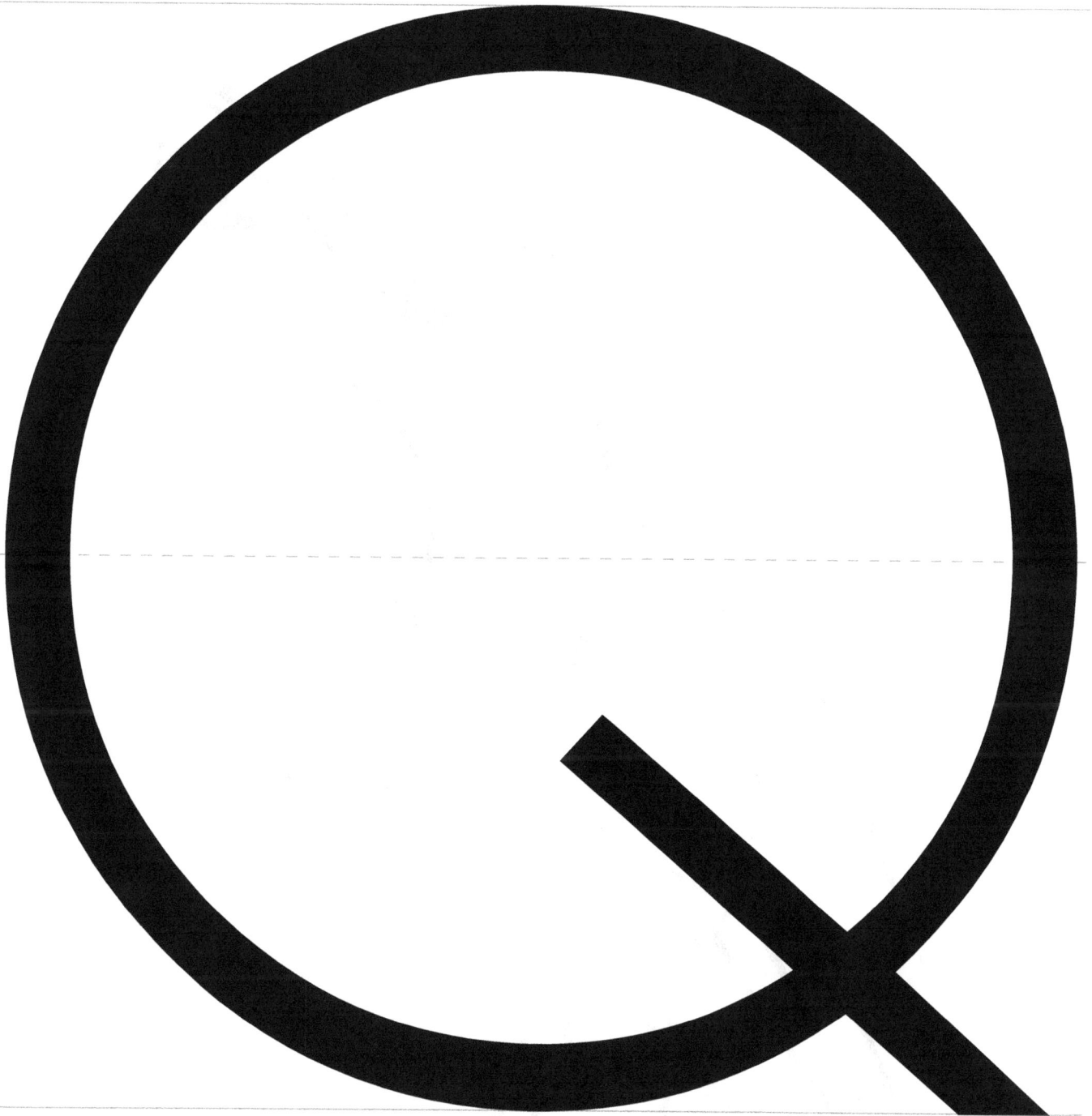

Trace the letters with a pencil.

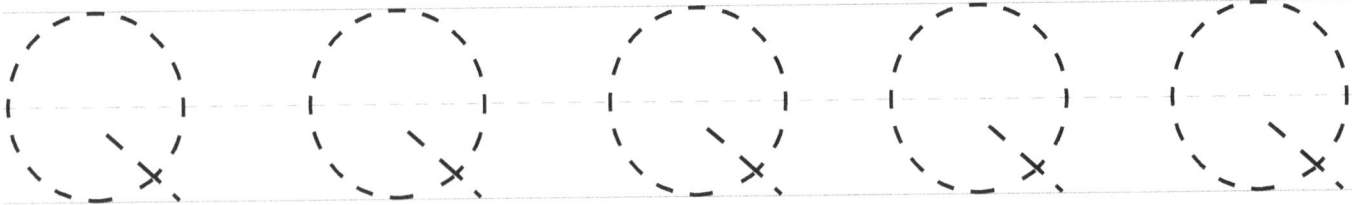

Color the Quail.

Trace Q and print your own letter Q four times with a pencil.

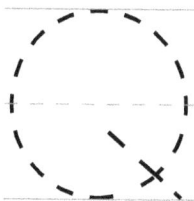

Draw a picture that starts with Q.

Demonstrate how to finger trace letter R.
Have child practice on the next page.

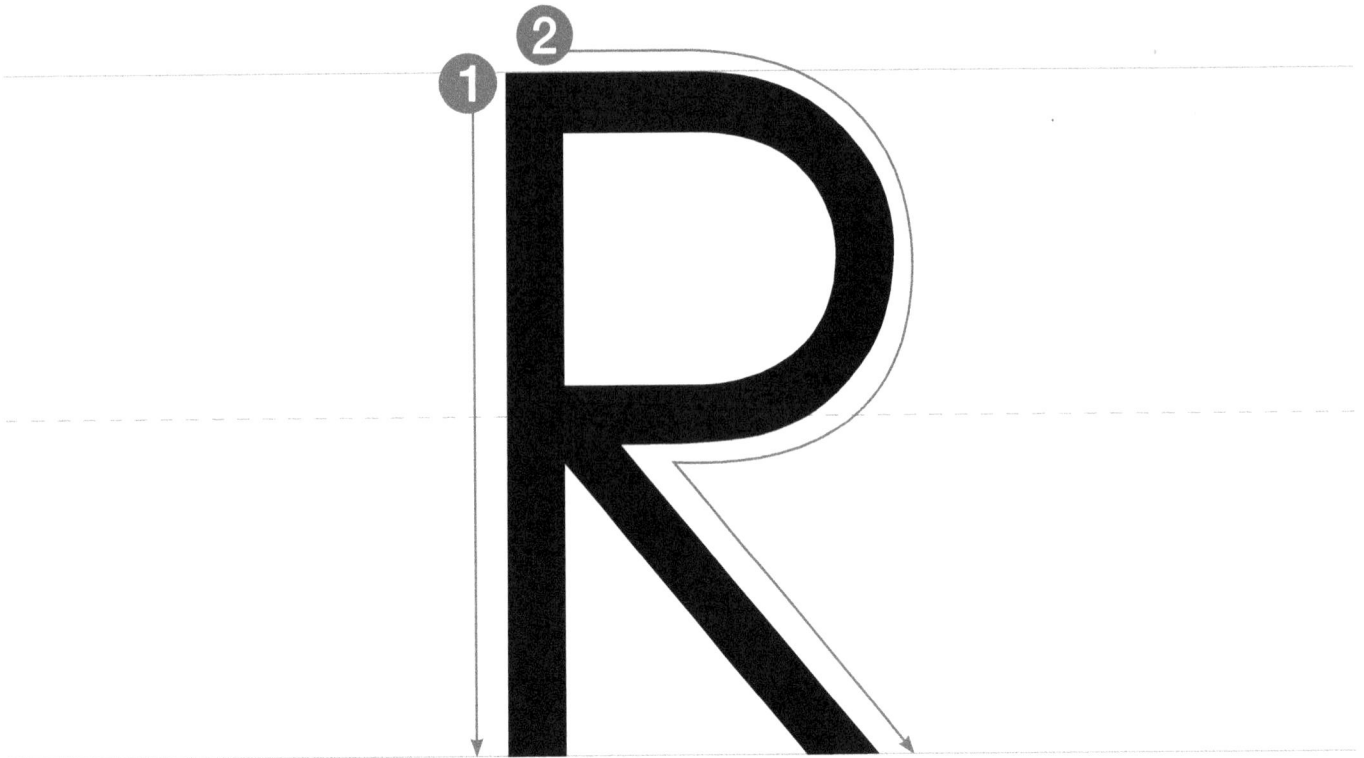

R

Directions:

1 Starting at the top go straight down.

Lift finger and bring back to the top.

2 Without lifting your finger curve around
to the middle and slant line down to bottom.

Say verbal clue when tracing R

**"DOWN ... AROUND TO MIDDLE ...
SLANT DOWN"**

Have child say verbal clue as they trace the letter with their finger
"DOWN ... AROUND TO MIDDLE ... SLANT DOWN"

R

Trace the letters with a pencil.

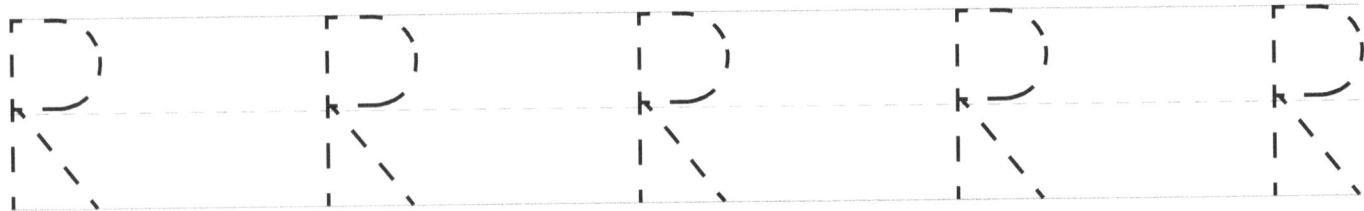

R R R R R

Color the Rooster.

Trace R and print your own letter R four times with a pencil.

R

Draw a picture that starts with R.

Demonstrate how to finger trace letter S.
Have child practice on the next page.

S ①

Directions:

① Starting below the top and without lifting your finger, circle left and up and around to middle (regular C), then circle right to the bottom (backward C).

Say verbal clue when tracing S

"REGULAR C ... BACKWARD C"

Have child say verbal clue as they trace the letter with their finger

"REGULAR C ... BACKWARD C"

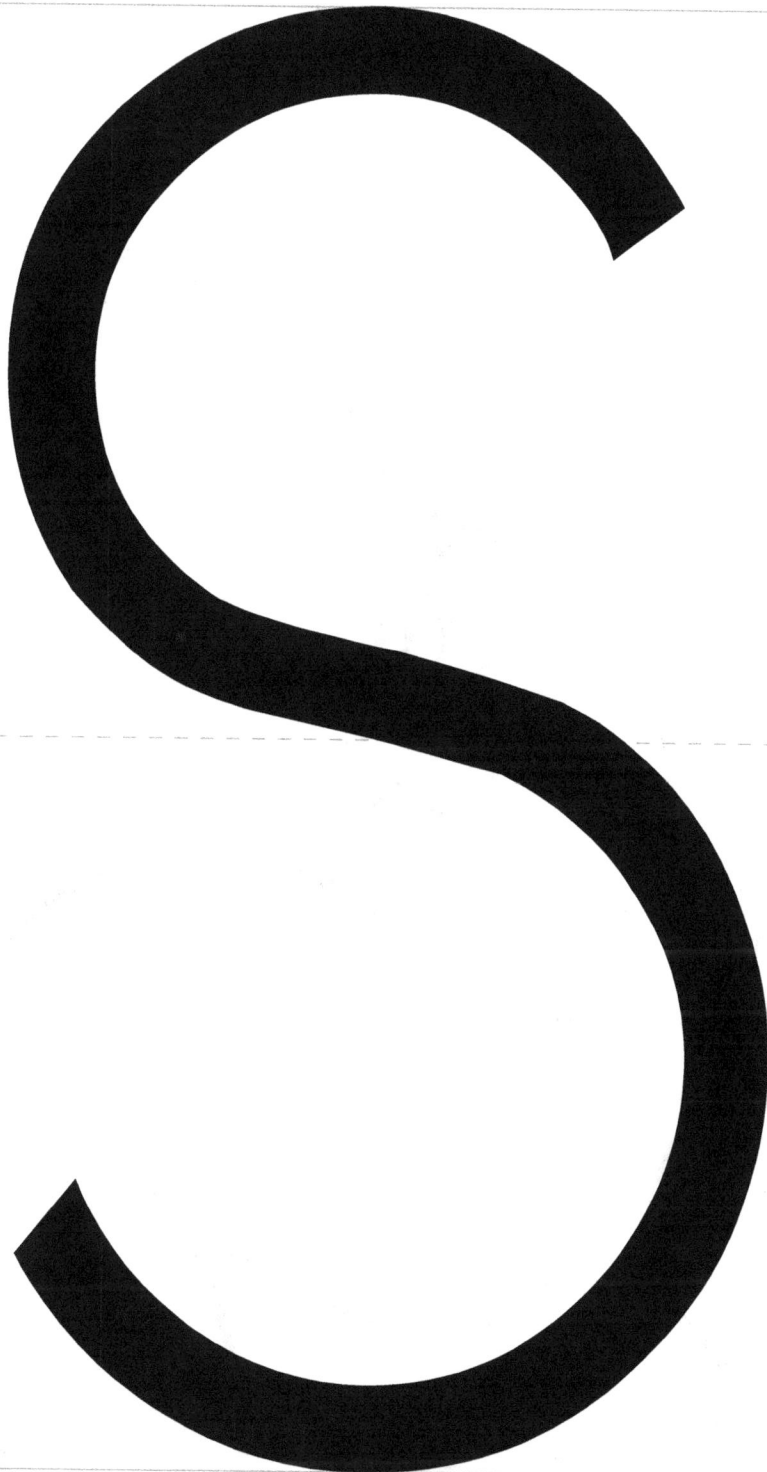

S

Trace the letters with a pencil.

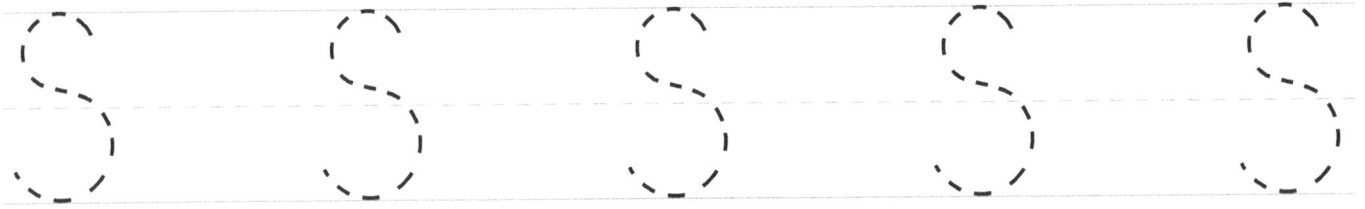

S   S   S   S   S

Color the Squirrel.

Trace S and print your own letter S four times with a pencil.

S

Draw a picture that starts with S.

Demonstrate how to finger trace letter T.
Have child practice on the next page.

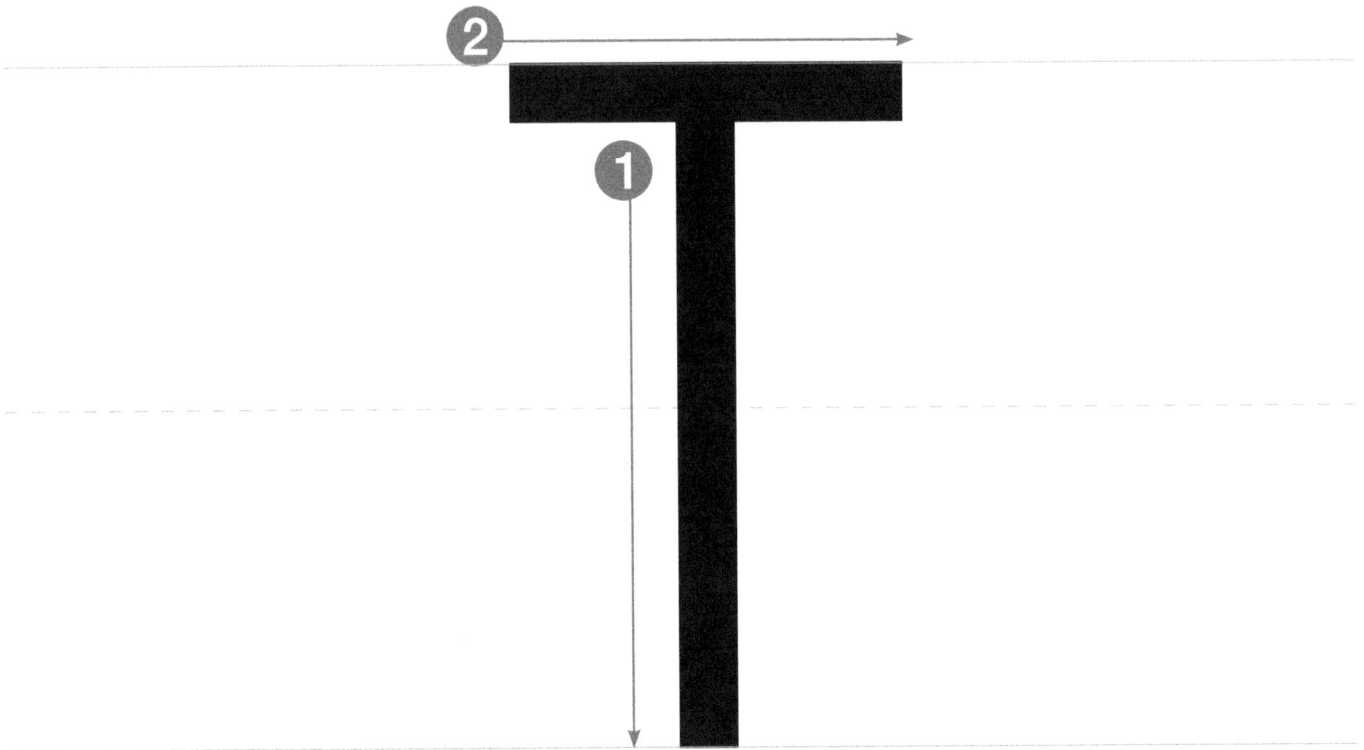

2 →

1

T

Directions:

1 Starting at the top go straight down.
Lift finger and bring back to the top.

2 Trace top line left to right.

Say verbal clue when tracing T
"DOWN ... TRACE TOP"

Have child say verbal clue as they trace the letter with their finger
"DOWN ... TRACE TOP"

Trace the letters with a pencil.

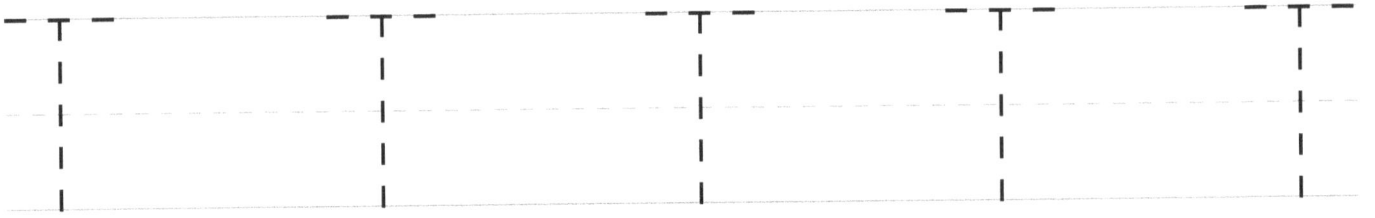

T T T T T

Color the Turtle.

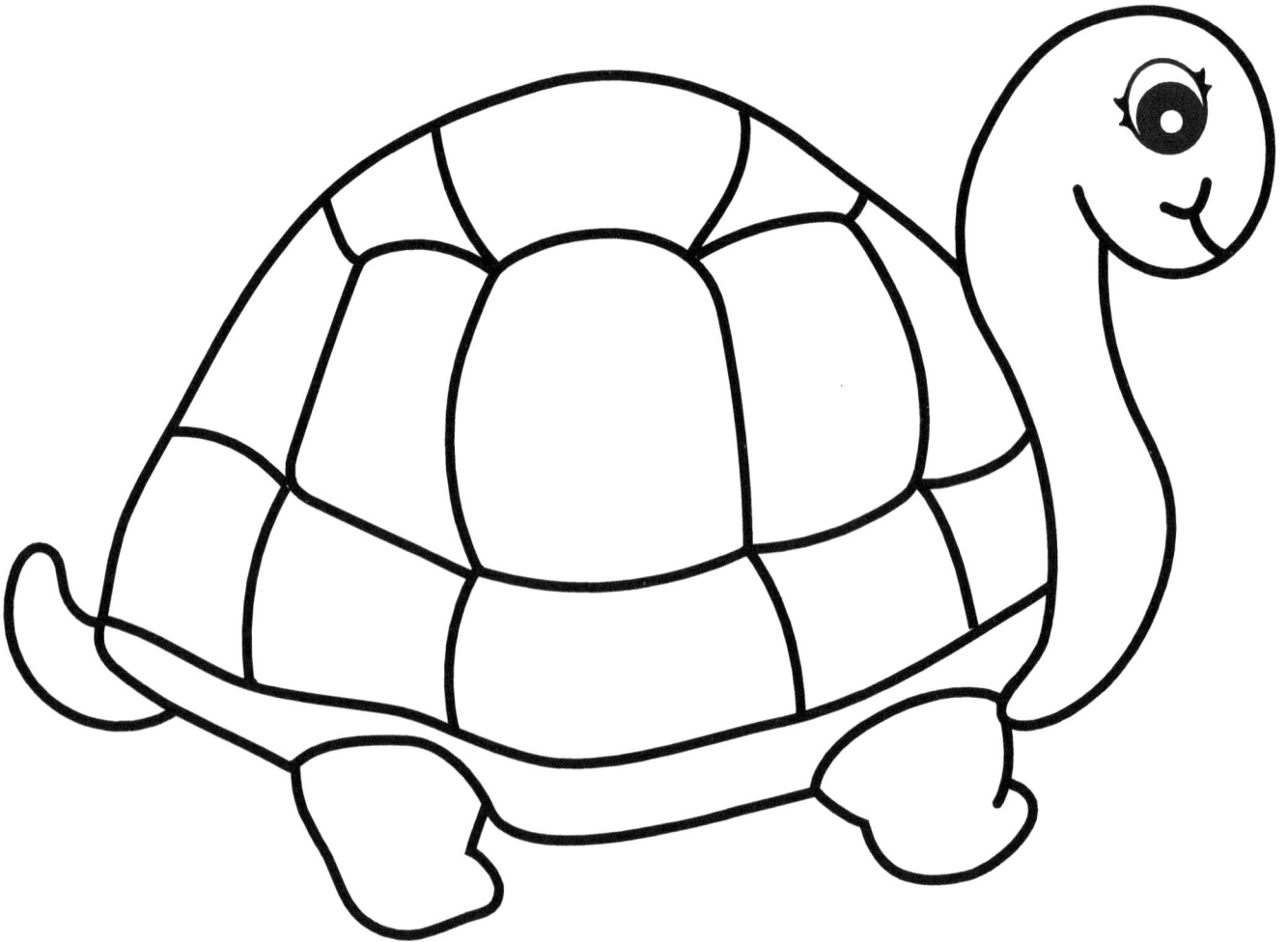

Trace T and print your own letter T four times with a pencil.

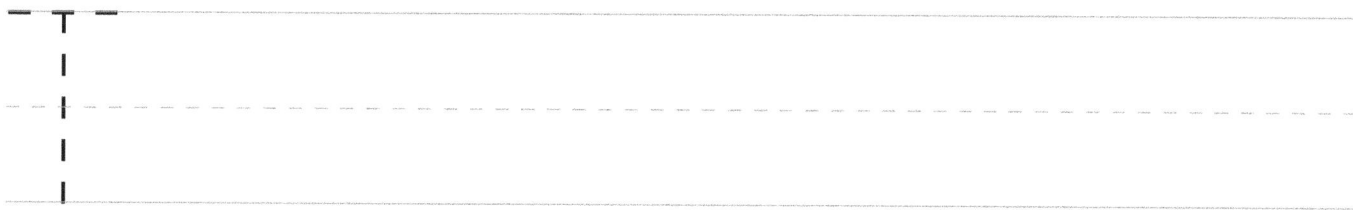

Draw a picture that starts with T.

Demonstrate how to finger trace letter U.
Have child practice on the next page.

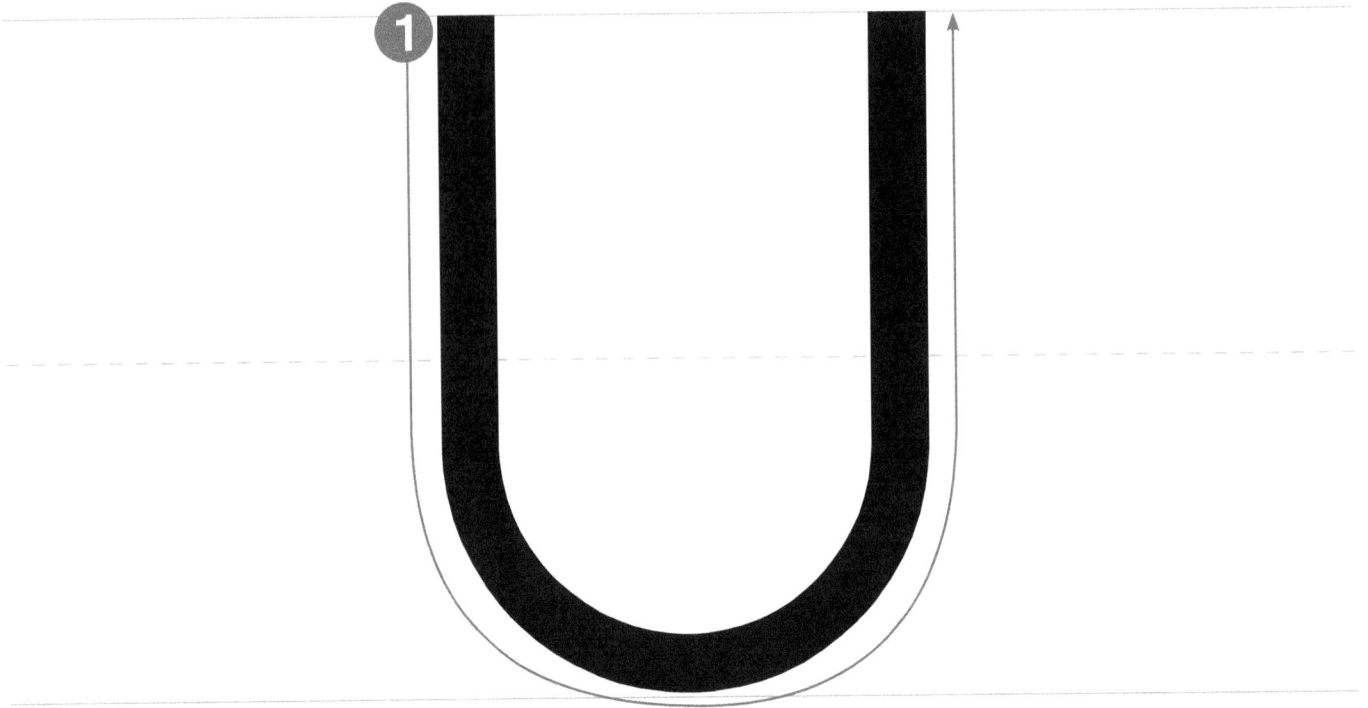

1

Directions:

1 Starting at the top and without lifting your finger go straight down, curve right and go straight back to top.

Say verbal clue when tracing U

"DOWN ... CURVE AROUND ... UP"

Have child say verbal clue as they trace the letter with their finger
"DOWN ... CURVE AROUND ... UP"

Trace the letters with a pencil.

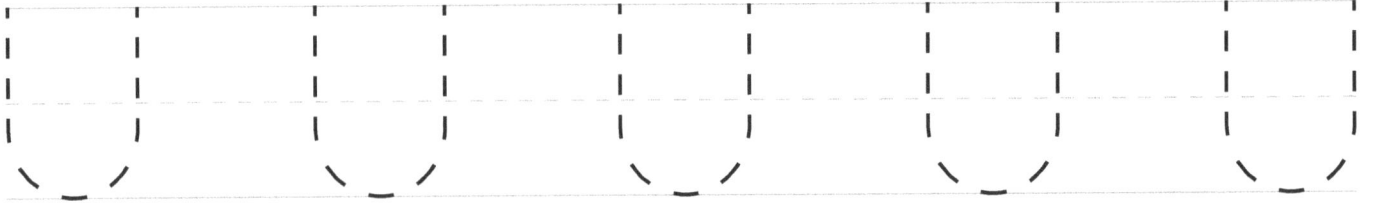

Color the Unicorn.

Trace U and print your own letter U four times with a pencil.

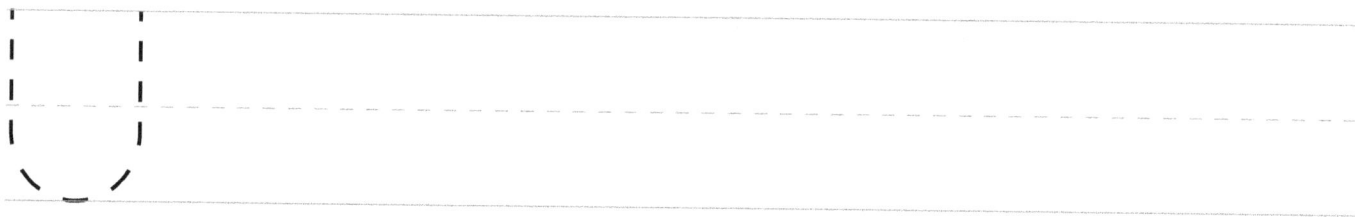

Draw a picture that starts with U.

Demonstrate how to finger trace letter V.
Have child practice on the next page.

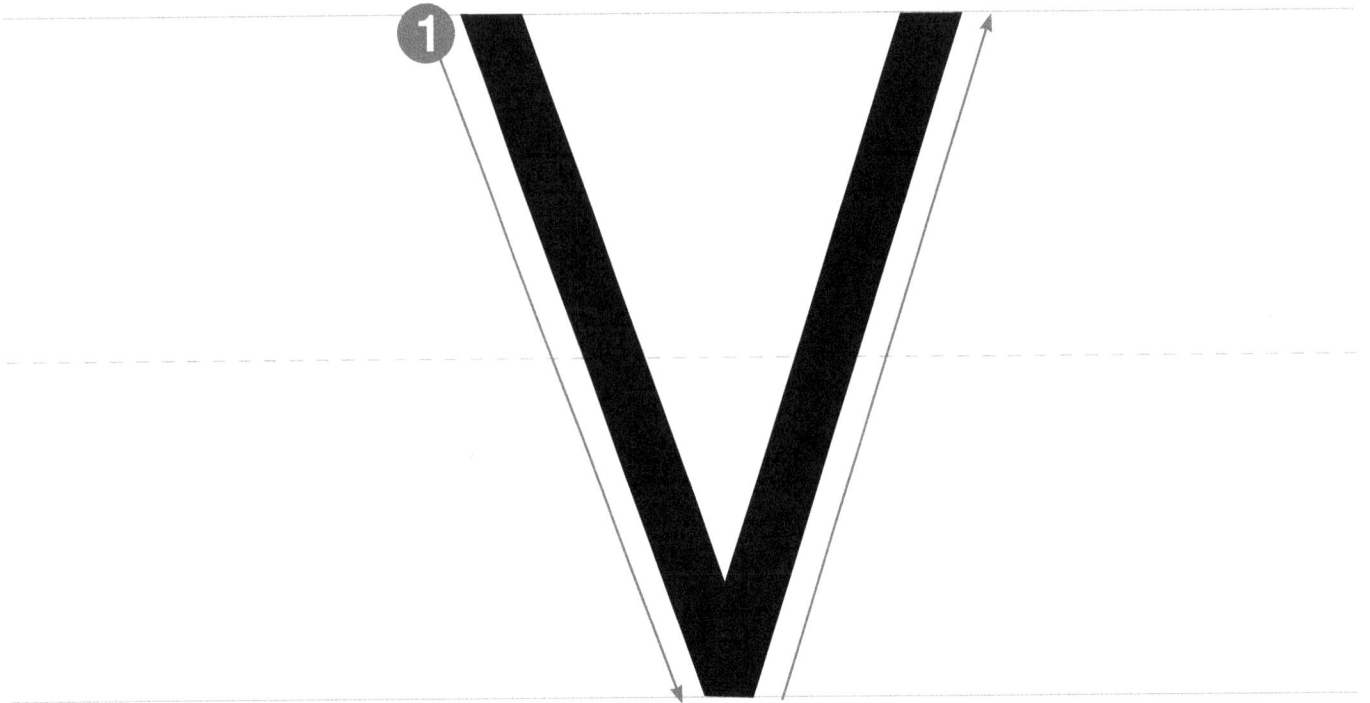

V

Directions:

1 Starting at the top and without lifting your finger, slant right to bottom and slant up to top.

Say verbal clue when tracing V
"SLANT DOWN ... SLANT UP"

Have child say verbal clue as they trace the letter with their finger
"SLANT DOWN ... SLANT UP"

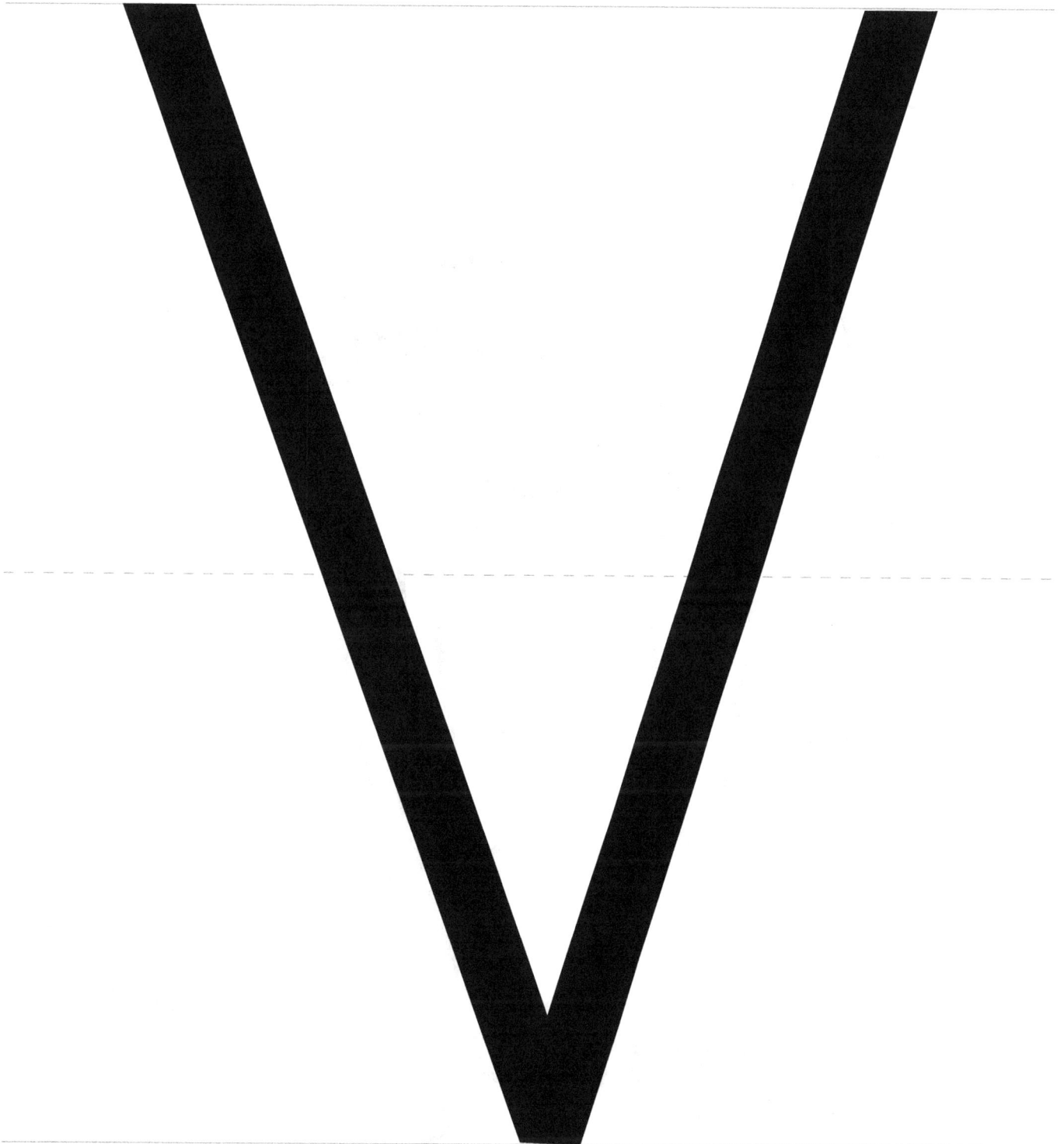

V

Trace the letters with a pencil.

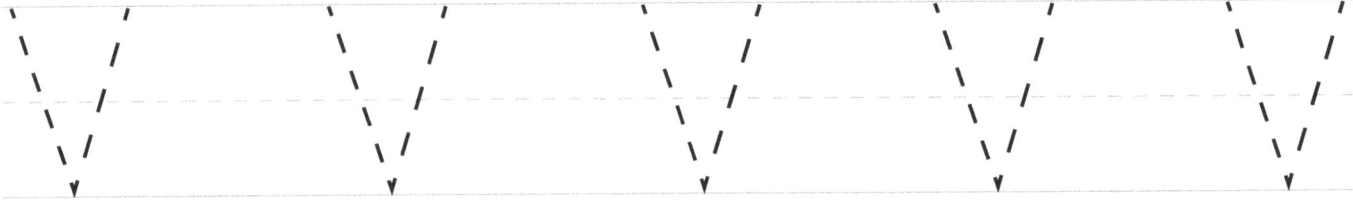

V V V V V

Color the Vulture.

Trace V and print your own letter V four times with a pencil.

V

Draw a picture that starts with V.

Demonstrate how to finger trace letter W.
Have child practice on the next page.

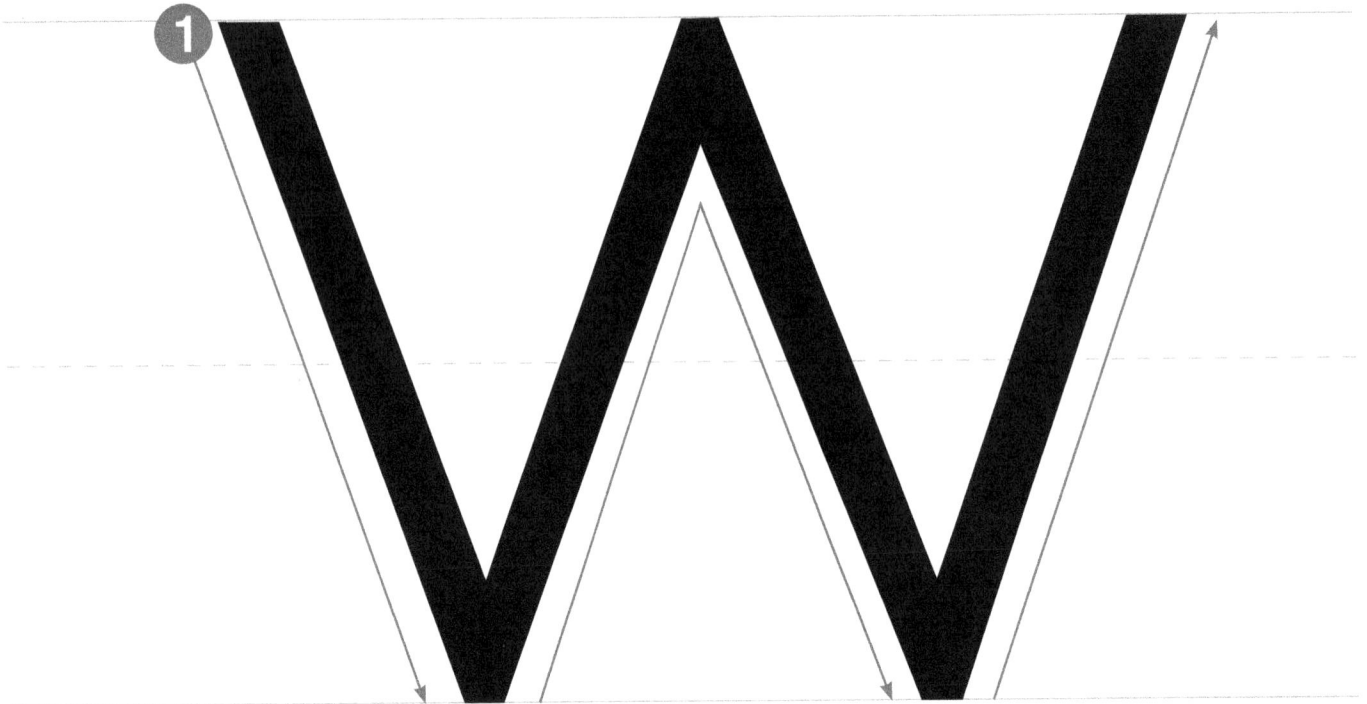

Directions:

1 Starting at the top and without lifting your finger, slant right to bottom, slant up to top, slant down to bottom, slant up to top.

Say verbal clue when tracing W

**"SLANT DOWN ... SLANT UP ...
SLANT DOWN ... SLANT UP"**

Have child say verbal clue as they trace the letter with their finger
"SLANT DOWN ... SLANT UP ... SLANT DOWN ... SLANT UP"

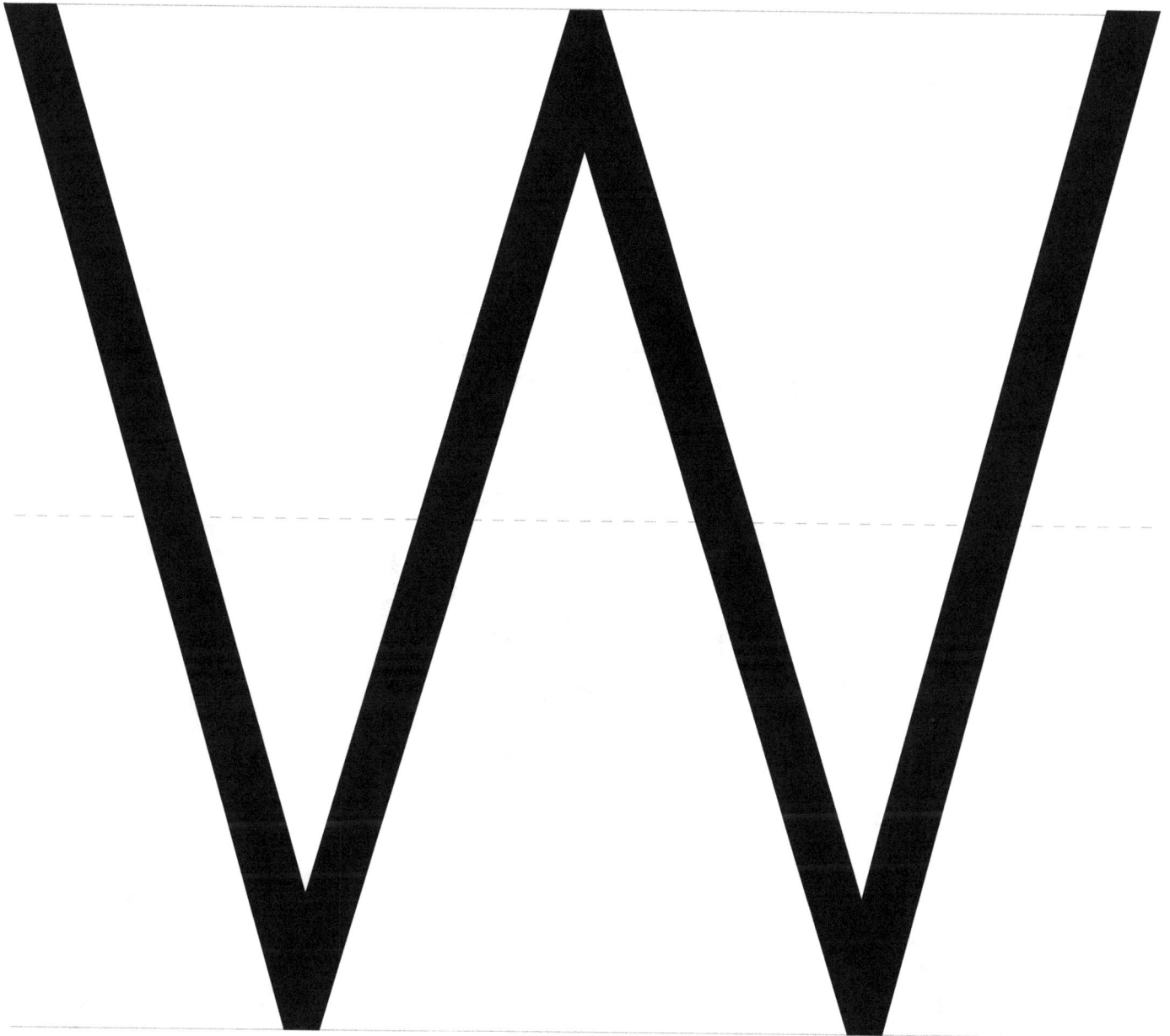

Trace the letters with a pencil.

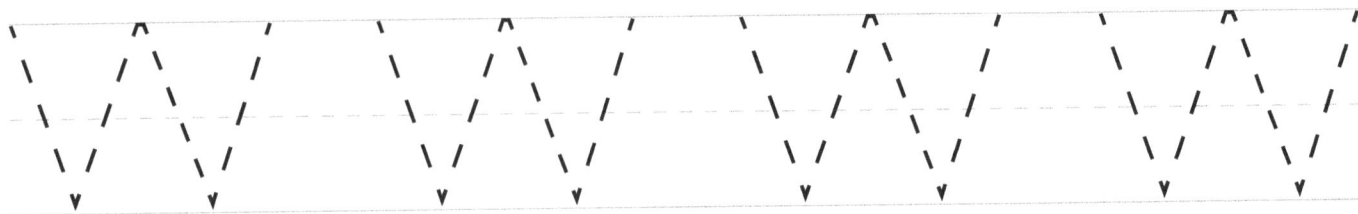

W W W W W

Color the Walrus.

Trace **W** and print your own letter **W** four times with a pencil.

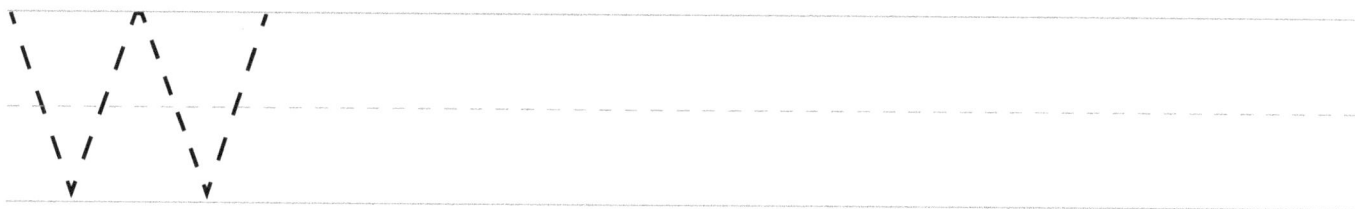

Draw a picture that starts with **W**.

Demonstrate how to finger trace letter X.
Have child practice on the next page.

X

Directions:

1. Starting at the top slant down right.
   Lift finger and bring back to the top..
2. Slant down left.

Say verbal clue when tracing X
"SLANT DOWN ... SLANT DOWN"

Have child say verbal clue as they trace the letter with their finger
"SLANT DOWN ... SLANT DOWN"

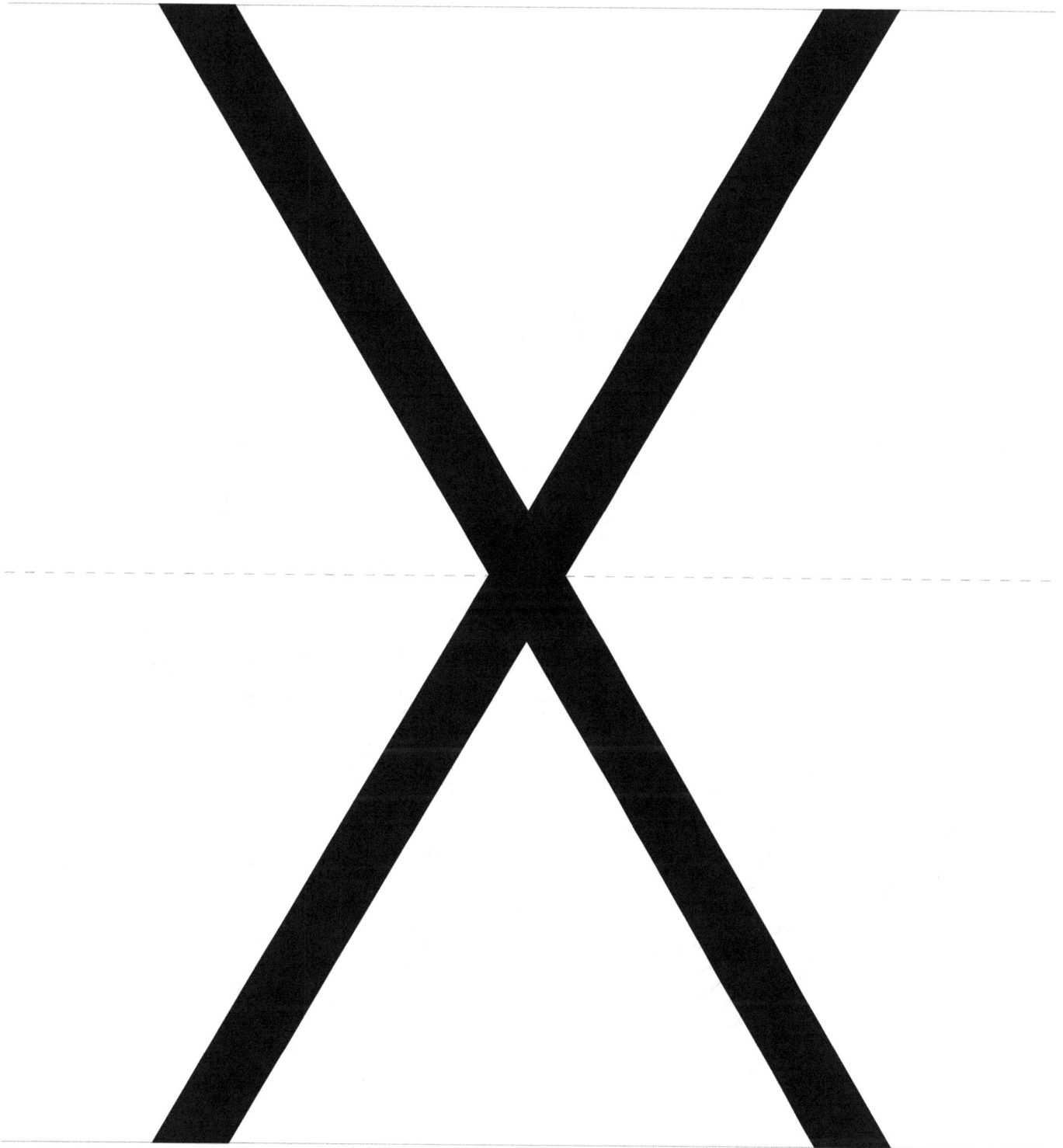

Trace the letters with a pencil.

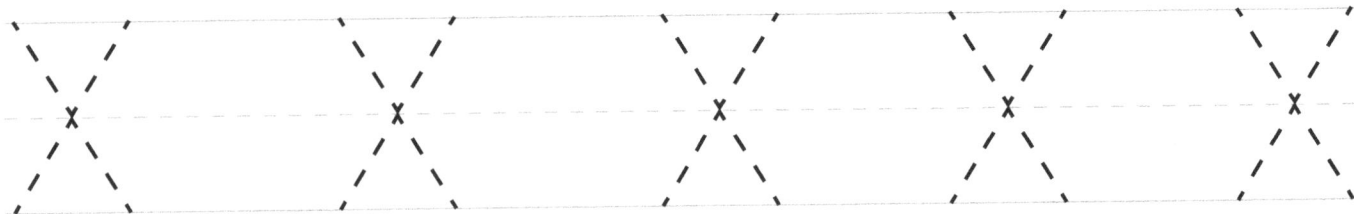

Color the X-Ray Fish.

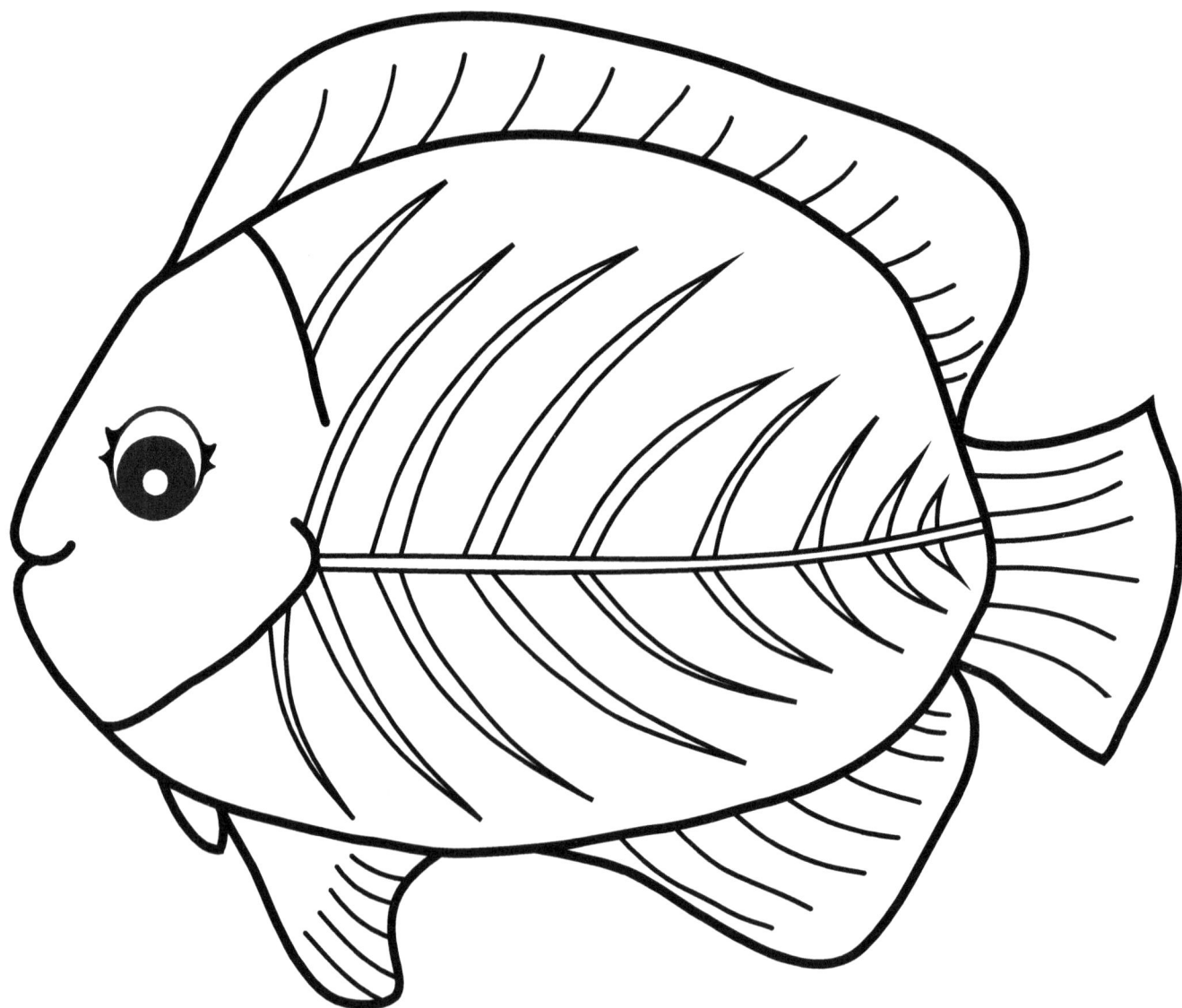

Trace X and print your own letter X four times with a pencil.

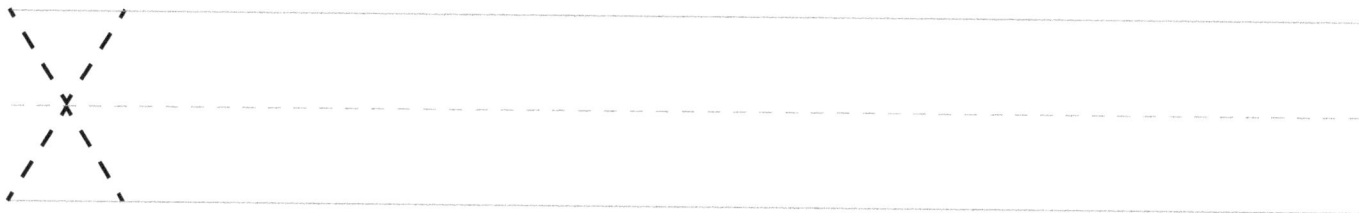

Draw a picture that starts with X.

Demonstrate how to finger trace letter Y.
Have child practice on the next page.

Directions:

1 Starting at the top slant right to middle.
Lift finger and bring back to the top.

2 Slant second line left to middle and then
straight down to bottom without lifting
your finger.

Say verbal clue when tracing Y
**"SLANT DOWN ... SLANT DOWN ...
STRAIGHT DOWN"**

Have child say verbal clue as they trace the letter with their finger
"SLANT DOWN ... SLANT DOWN ... STRAIGHT DOWN"

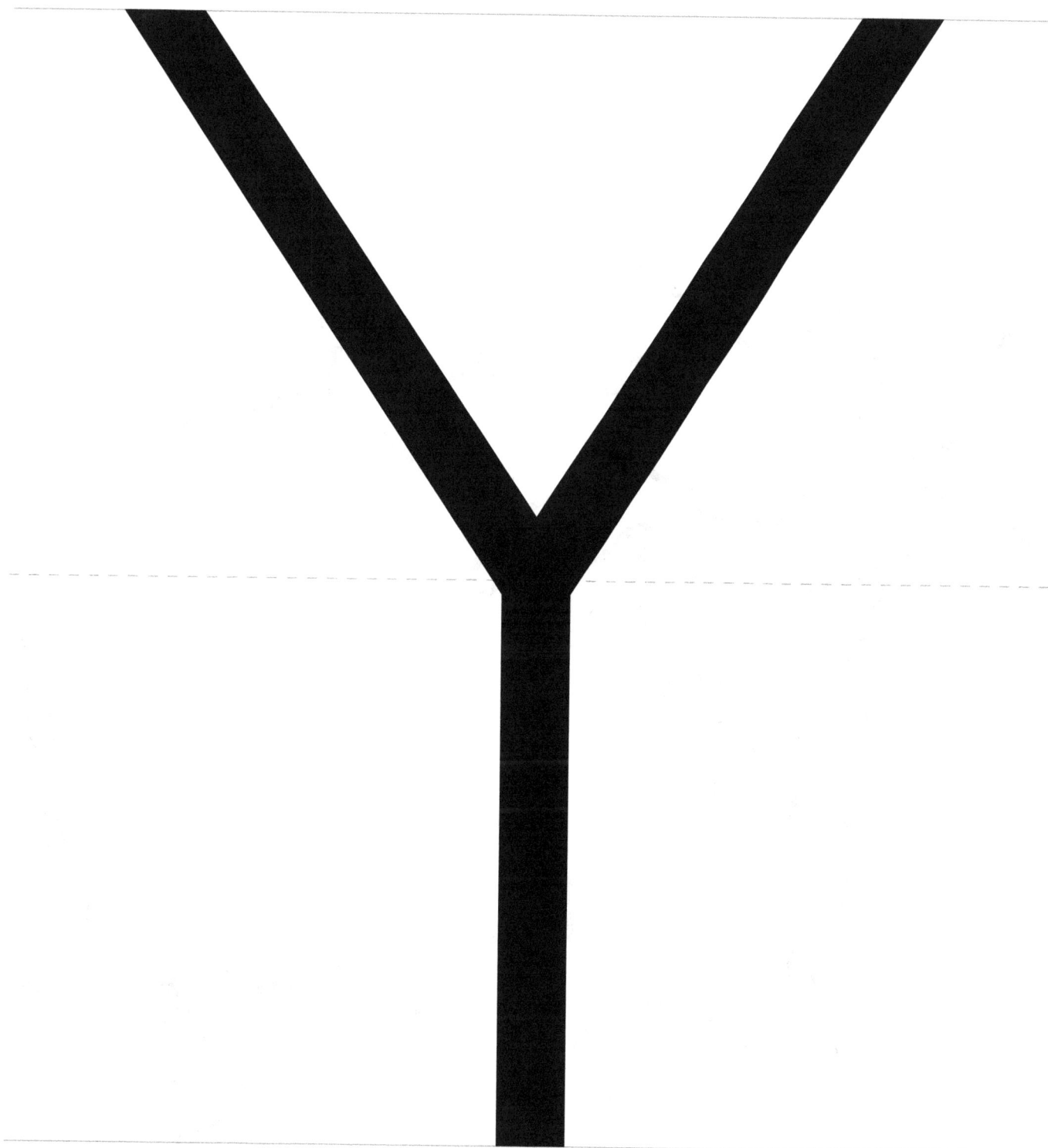

Trace the letters with a pencil.

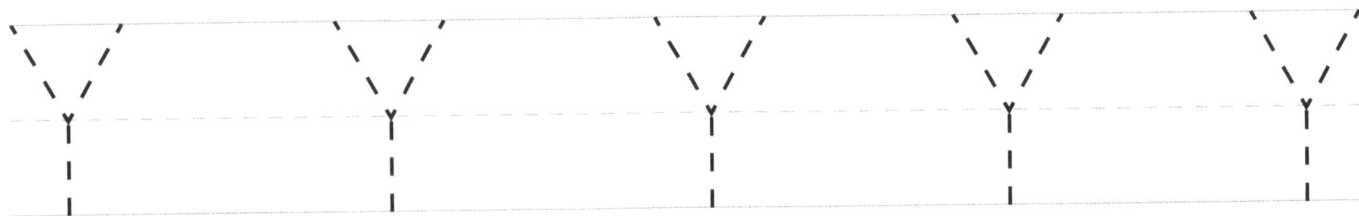

Y Y Y Y Y

Color the Yak.

Trace Y and print your own letter Y four times with a pencil.

Y

Draw a picture that starts with Y.

Demonstrate how to finger trace letter Z.
Have child practice on the next page.

1

Z

Directions:

1 Starting at the top and without lifting
your finger trace top line to the right,
slant down left, trace bottom line
to the right.

Say verbal clue when tracing Z
**"TRACE TOP ... SLANT DOWN ...
TRACE BOTTOM"**

Have child say verbal clue as they trace the letter with their finger
"TRACE TOP ... SLANT DOWN ... TRACE BOTTOM"

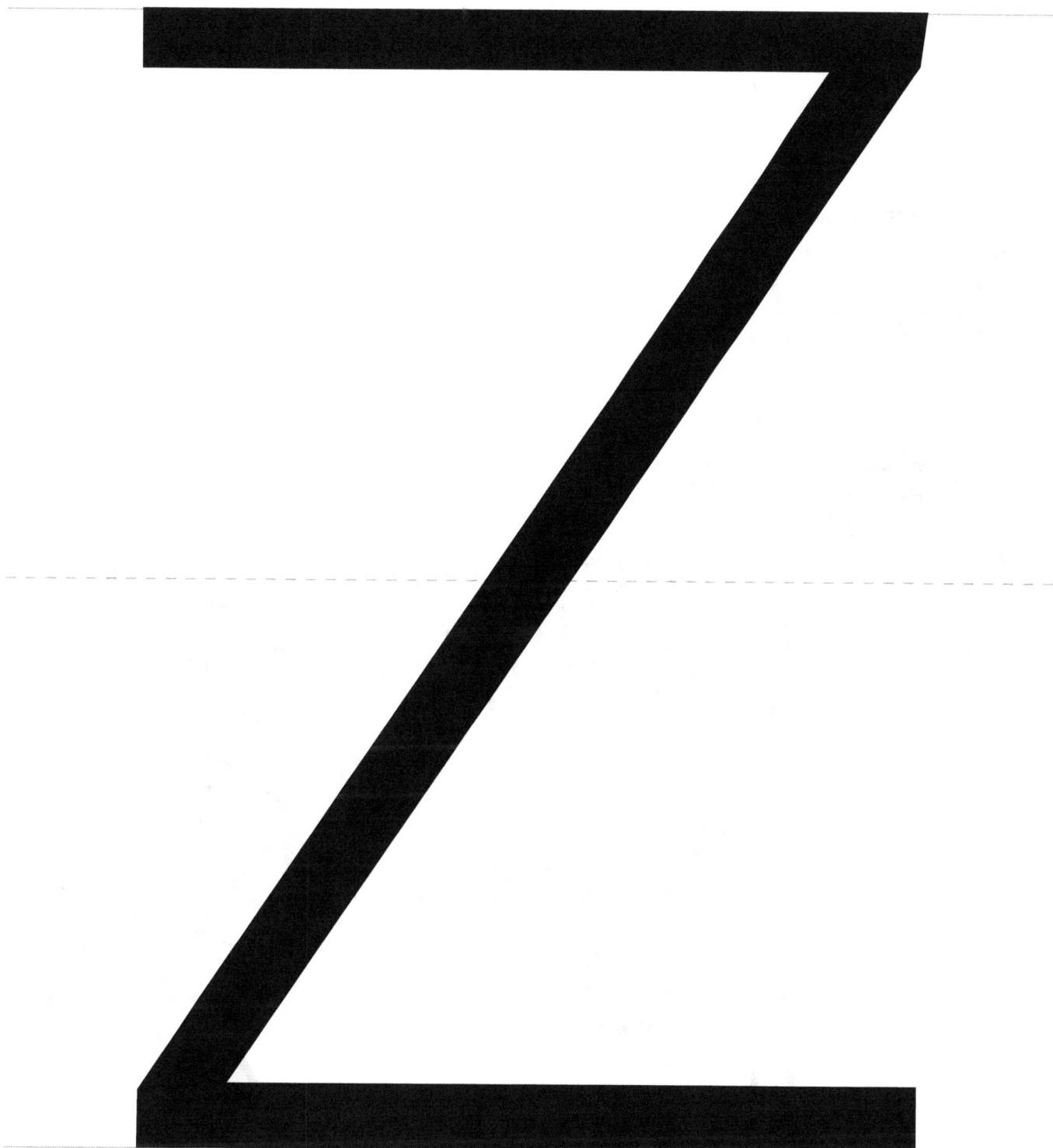

Trace the letters with a pencil.

Color the Zebra.

Trace Z and print your own letter Z four times with a pencil.

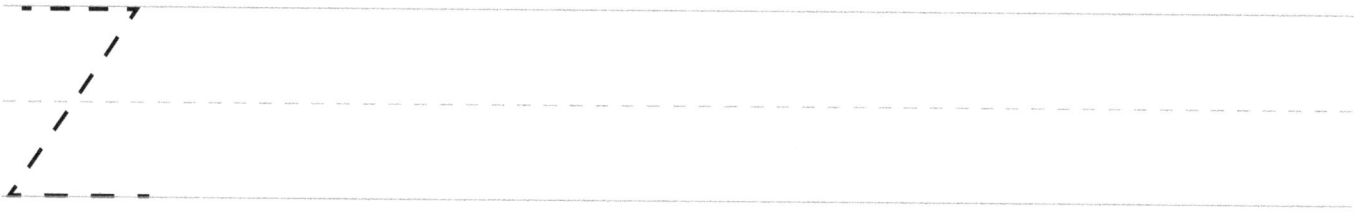

Draw a picture that starts with Z.

Verbal Clues For Uppercase Letters

A — "DOWN ... DOWN ... CONNECT"

B — "DOWN ... BACK TO THE TOP ... AROUND ... AROUND"

C — "CIRCLE UP AND AROUND BUT DON'T CLOSE"

D — "DOWN ... BACK TO THE TOP ... AROUND"

E — "DOWN ... TRACE TOP ... TRACE MIDDLE ... TRACE BOTTOM"

F — "DOWN ... TRACE TOP ... TRACE MIDDLE"

G — "CIRCLE UP AND AROUND ... THEN IN"

H — "DOWN ... DOWN ... CONNECT"

I — "DOWN ... TRACE TOP ... TRACE BOTTOM"

J — "DOWN ... CURVE ... TRACE TOP"

K — "DOWN ... SLANT IN ... SLANT OUT"

L — "DOWN ... TRACE BOTTOM"

M — "DOWN ... SLANT DOWN ... SLANT UP ... STRAIGHT DOWN"

N   "STRAIGHT DOWN ... SLANT DOWN ... STRAIGHT UP"

O   "CIRCLE UP AND AROUND TO CLOSE"

P   "DOWN ... BACK TO THE TOP ... AROUND TO MIDDLE"

Q   "CIRCLE UP AND AROUND TO CLOSE ... ADD SLANTED LINE"

R   "DOWN ... AROUND TO MIDDLE ... SLANT DOWN"

S   "REGULAR C ... BACKWARD C"

T   "DOWN ... TRACE TOP"

U   "DOWN ... CURVE AROUND ... UP"

V   "SLANT DOWN ... SLANT UP"

W   "SLANT DOWN ... SLANT UP ... SLANT DOWN ... SLANT UP"

X   "SLANT DOWN ... SLANT DOWN"

Y   "SLANT DOWN ... SLANT DOWN ... STRAIGHT DOWN"

Z   "TRACE TOP ... SLANT DOWN ... TRACE BOTTOM"

www.ingramcontent.com/pod-product-compliance
Lightning Source LLC
Chambersburg PA
CBHW081256040426
42452CB00014B/2531